The Perfectly Imperfect Mum

The Perfectly Imperfect Mum

JOANNE MITCHELL

THE CHOIR PRESS

First published in the United Kingdom in 2017 by
The Choir Press

ISBN 978-1-910864-88-3

Contents

Dedication

To my special dad, who so loved to listen to the stories and antics my friends and I got up to. Once our own children came along, there were more of us and many more stories, and he always used to say to us:

'You should write a book, you lot.'

An Introduction

Well here it is, Dad.

I feel sure he's been by my side whilst I have been writing, giving me a nudge here and there when I've needed it. So, as he would have said, just enjoy.

This, I think you'll find, is a book with a difference. I'm definitely no scholar, as you'll soon realise after reading just a few pages. Spelling and punctuation have haunted me throughout my life. However, I have always loved to write letters, diaries and poems. So I decided that, despite all the odds being against me, I was going to attempt to write a book.

Everything I've written is entirely true, to as much detail as I can remember. When the idea first came to me of what I was going to write about, I did think that I might have to elaborate the truth slightly, to perhaps make it more interesting to you, the reader. Once everything started coming together and fitting into place though, I really didn't feel this was necessary. So I've left all the events exactly as they happened.

It's been helped very much on its way with a great deal of input from my two fantastic children, Abbie and James, plus Daniel, Abbie's boyfriend, who, fortunately for me, are all extremely clever when it comes to English grammar. I started to put pen to paper back in April 2014, determined, much to everyone's disbelief, to prove you don't necessarily have to be fantastic at English to write a book. If the words are inside you, all you have to do is get them out on to paper and with a little – or in my case, a lot of – help, you're on your way. That said, my punctuation and spelling of many words has entertained both family and friends for as long as I can remember, resulting in a good few 'Joanne-isms' now being added to our vocabulary. As the book has reached finalisation many of them sadly have had to be removed. You may also notice a hint of Yorkshire dialect in the writing here and there, but as a Yorkshire girl born and bred, this was also something else we felt needed to be left in. So, that's all my apologies and excuses out of the way.

Before you start the story, I'd just like to draw your attention to some wonderful people who have helped me along the way.

Thank you to my English teacher (if you're still alive). Although I never appeared to be listening in your class, I hope this book goes some way towards helping you to feel your time was not completely wasted on me.

Thank you, also, to my amazing children, Abbie and James, as without them this book would not have been possible.

Firstly, I wouldn't have had anything to write about, and secondly, without their knowledge of the English language it would never have been fit for publication. I'd really like to tell you that they've been so patient with me and my lack of computer skills, but they definitely have not. Like all of today's generation, who have been using computers since they were babies, it's difficult for them to comprehend why us grown-ups have little – or in my case zero – knowledge of how to use one, so they found it much easier and less painful to just do it for me. Consequently, my abilities at the computer have not dramatically increased since writing this … although after starting to write with the trusty pen and paper back in 2014, I'm extremely pleased to tell you that by page seven I was able to turn the computer on, all by myself. This was of course all good and well until something went wrong and perhaps on occasions I accidentally pressed a button that I didn't mean to, often resulting in me spending whole days writing in different fonts, in the wrong colour, and at least once I underlined something and then didn't know how to make it stop. The kids found it highly amusing arriving home from school to find I'd written four whole pages and it was all underlined, like an extremely over-ambitious heading. On more than one occasion a potential full day's writing has been lost, all due to my fear of pressing a wrong button and deleting the whole book.

They found it very amusing at first that Mum was attempting to write anything, but as I battled on and they realised I was determined to do it, they've spent endless hours helping me and correcting my spelling and punctuation mistakes.

My sister, who herself is an author, has guided me a great deal; she's sat for hours, chuckling at my different approach to book writing. I have great admiration for the very brave and patient proofreaders, the pre-proofreaders and the pre-pre-proofreaders, as that's how many times it's taken my mum and her partner, Michael, to help me put the finishing touches to this book.

I must mention Miles at The Choir Press and Meg, who definitely drew the short straw being assigned to be the editor of my book. Both have been tremendously kind, helpful and tolerant.

Not forgetting a huge thank you to Harry Forde, who has drawn my amazing cover picture. Although in the middle of his A Levels himself, he has taken the time to do this for me.

I am eternally grateful to you all ...

The house has been a mess and we've eaten strange concoctions of food at odd times of the day, but we all survived, and are still here to tell the tale, as it were. My husband Gary was initially rather shocked to hear of my plans to write a book, but he's always encouraged me to keep going, often retuning home after three days working away to no tea ready and a very empty fridge. He's never complained once; instead, he has just quietly taken himself off to the supermarket and left me to it.

Thank you to you, the reader, for taking the time to read this. I hope it brings a smile to your face and helps to lighten up your own journey through parenthood.

The Perfect Mum?

So you have no idea who I am, do you? Well, according to my fourteen-year-old son, today I am the perfect mum.

Now, that could have something to do with the fact that I have just returned home from the supermarket loaded down with Coco Pops, a large 'to share' bag of Doritos, which he almost certainly won't be sharing, and a family size box of Maltesers. These are for him and his three friends who are sleeping over tonight – and so soon after our chat the previous evening about how important it is for him to start making the healthy choice when choosing his food.

'You are what you eat, James,' I'd said.

I'd pondered at the fresh fruit, salad and vegetable aisle for quite some time that afternoon, thinking that if I cut everything up and put it into colour-coordinated dishes, maybe they would go for it. But who was I trying to kid? They're fourteen, for goodness' sake. So I went with my original plan and stocked up with plenty of pizzas, fizzy drinks, crisps and sweets.

1
Just so you know

I'd left school aged fifteen, which was basically as soon as I possibly could. I couldn't wait to leave – since the age of five I had told my parents that I was going to be a hairdresser when I grew up. Amazingly, when I was thirteen, my mum and dad purchased a small hair salon, with living accommodation above. I couldn't believe it. This was so exciting for me – my dream really was coming true.

Shortly after moving in I started to work there every spare moment I could, rushing home from school each evening to ensure I could help out before they closed. I worked every school holiday I could and always managed the 6.30am start on a Saturday. I was soon to become a master in tea and coffee making, taking customer's coats and getting them gowned up, all ready for their hair treatments and, of course, the endless job of sweeping up all the hair. After three months of that, shampooing training finally began. I was in heaven – at last, I was let loose on real people. On my very first Saturday, after having shampooed the three early morning ladies at 6.30 (with a couple emerging from the basin just a little wet!) I then sat down to have a rest on the backwash chair whilst I awaited my next victim. Apparently, only moments later, I was fast asleep.

When the salon closed on a Saturday lunchtime, I'd bring my Girls' World Styling Head downstairs, strap it on to a broom and tie the broom to the back of one of the salon chairs so I could pretend it was a real person and I was a real hairdresser. Whilst cutting the Girls' World head's hair I'd also be having a full-on conversation with her. Having all net curtains in the window meant that nobody could see in – let's hope they couldn't anyway. I was just counting down the days until I could finally leave school and start at hairdressing college.

Now, finding out that I didn't need any qualifications to get into hairdressing college probably was the best news for me. That, added to the fact that I'd most definitely have a job on leaving school, meant that I could do even less work whilst at school than I already had been doing, if that was at all humanly possible. You see, I used this knowledge to its full potential and although I made great friends and spent a lot of time having fun, I learnt very little during my time at school. I did, however, take on the role of being class clown and, if I do say so myself, I made quite a good job of it, managing to annoy most of my teachers whilst keeping the rest of the class entertained. I would often return home on an evening with white hair from where the teacher had thrown the blackboard eraser at my head. He did get to be a rather good shot, possibly due to the fact that I gave him plenty of opportunities to practise his aim.

I wasn't necessarily a naughty child at school – I just found it hard to stop talking, and the more people laughed at me the more I would carry on talking. There wasn't many a day went by that I didn't spend at least some of my time standing outside the classroom, usually facing the wall. But as long as my parents didn't ever find out about this, I knew I was safe. Had my behaviour been brought to their attention, I don't think I would have been here today to tell the tale, because their strict-but-fair upbringing had taught me that some things were best kept away from them. This was definitely one thing that would be better if it remained a secret. Unfortunately for me, they didn't give out grades for the best clown in the class, otherwise I'm sure an A* would have been coming my way. So it was no surprise that when I did finally finish school, I left with only three exams passed: Drama, Art and Cookery.

Well, what more did I need? I was ready to face the world now, wasn't I?

2

Leaving Yorkshire

I worked five days a week in my parents' salon, then on Mondays (my day off) I went into college. It was here that I met Stacey, when we were fifteen. At first I kept my distance from her and watched from afar, as she was a larger-than-life character and, to be quite honest, she scared me a little. We actually didn't become good friends until we were about eighteen. Having both been in long relationships since the age of fifteen, we then suddenly found ourselves single at roughly the same time. This was when I got to meet the real Stacey, and I discovered that underneath the larger-than-life character was really quite a nervous girl who was going through far more than I could ever imagine at home. Both her parents were struggling with ill health, her dad battling with Parkinson's disease whilst her mum, a long-term sufferer of ME, was finding nursing him at home almost impossible. Stacey's two older brothers no longer lived at home, leaving her pretty much running the home and caring for both parents. Amazingly, she'd bounce into college week after week with a smile on her face and entertain the whole group with her dry sense of humour and quick wit.

Being single was new to both of us. We suddenly had a lot in common and, more importantly, a lot to learn. The initial excitement of spending our only day off at hairdressing college soon wore thin, so we replaced the odd lesson or two with a visit to the pub over the road. This gave us much more time to talk about organising our holidays abroad without being interrupted by the teachers.

As the years went by Stacey and I travelled together a lot, starting off with a week's holiday in Majorca, where we promised ourselves that one day we'd return and stay for much longer. True to our word, when we were both twenty-one we did just that. We decided to pack in our jobs and travel the world!

Well, the world did seem a little daunting, so back to Majorca it was, as we figured this was a good place to start. We'd been saving up for over a year, so we now had enough money to pay for our flights and accommodation once we arrived. Knowing that the money wouldn't last for long, we knew that we were going to have to get ourselves a job to allow us to stay out there for any length of time. Our initial idea was to go there as hairdressers with our new skills; however, there wasn't much call for hairdressers without work permits – a small detail we seemed to have overlooked. We then turned our skills to bar touting instead. I'm sorry to say that our first job was as two of those annoying people who stand outside bars abroad. I'm sure you know the ones I mean – they try to convince holiday makers that their bar is better than all the rest, usually offering two-for-the-price-of-one deals on all the drinks. So we would start work at 9pm and finish around 1am. We didn't bring in a great deal of money for our employer, however, because he'd hinted to us that what we were doing wasn't entirely legal. Therefore, Stacey and I did spend quite a chunk of our working hours hiding behind trees, avoiding the local police whilst they did their nightly patrols. It wasn't too long either before our boss realised that we were actually drinking far more than we were selling. So after only about three weeks working at the Charing Cross Bar, he bade us farewell.

Now unemployed, we'd heard on the grapevine that we could make some money by selling the tickets for our return flights home. As we weren't going to need them, we thought that this was a good idea and decided to give it a go in a process whereby we went to the airport with the people who were buying our tickets from us. All we had to do was go to the checking-in desk with them and check them in with our passports, as in those days this was the only time the tickets and passports were shown together. We then handed over our tickets to them and they were away. It was that simple – a far cry from today's much tighter security, I hear you say. Yes, indeed, it seems impossible to imagine that it was as easy as that back then. The cash we made on the flight tickets put a little money back into the pot, but we knew we would have to get some more work soon, to enable us to stay out there for longer.

We were offered several jobs in our time there, ranging from selling marijuana to topless mud-wrestling. I'm extremely pleased to say we accepted neither, although we did contemplate the topless mud-wrestling, but when we were told it would be against each other, I flatly refused as there was no way I could have hit Stacey. Instead we decided to share our accommodation with some other travellers that we'd made good friends with. This kept the cost of living down and meant our money lasted much longer. Between us we took on an odd job here and there, but our main jobs were really sunbathing and going out.

As we were locals now, we did tend to get a few free drinks in a lot of the bars, and after 1am in Banana's Nightclub we could have up to five free drinks. This often meant that we couldn't quite make the journey all the way back to our apartment and as the sun was usually beginning to rise by this time, a sunbed on the beach would suffice. That was, until the beach started to fill up with tommy tourists, as we called them, at which point we knew that the sunbed man would soon be coming around and wanting some money for our beds, a luxury we couldn't afford. Then it was time to head back to Apartment 7E, which we now shared with five other travellers, sleeping for most of the day to ensure we could do it all again that night. We'd made some great friends and our one-bedroomed apartment with seven mattresses on the floor soon became home for us all.

There were some very nice hotels around and one or two of them had started to use a new system called all-inclusive. This, as you will now know well, is where you pay for all your food and drink before your holiday. It was still in the experimental period in the nineties and we'd noticed a flaw in the way it worked as there seemed to be no real way of staff knowing if you were staying in the hotel or not when it came to mealtimes. This gave us a great idea: we would often go along to one of them for our breakfast and simply join the end of the queue like everyone else who was a guest at the hotel. Then we'd fill our plates with some of the best food we'd seen in a long time, often enjoying a full English with all the trimmings. I do believe that now in all-inclusive hotels, you do have to wear a recognisable wristband at all times. I'm not sure, but perhaps this may have something to do with us.

As money was very tight for us all in 7E it was a big luxury for us to eat something other than eggy bread, beans on toast or pasta. This had become our staple diet as this was all we could afford, although every Saturday night we did look forward to our treat: a packet of chocolate digestive biscuits, which was shared between us all. Splitting the shopping bill between the seven of us did have its downsides, as having one bar of soap, one deodorant and one tube of toothpaste could cause some friction when everyone was trying to get ready to go out. It was all worthwhile, as keeping ourselves on a tight budget enabled us to stay there for a good eight weeks, after which the money was beginning to run out and we had to then start thinking about returning back home. This would require some tickets and as we'd sold ours on, we now needed to buy ourselves some more from other travellers who weren't needing their return tickets just yet.

Once we'd found ourselves two suitable passengers with return flights back to Yorkshire, we offered what we believed to be a suitable price for them, which they gladly accepted. So the tough job of packing up and saying our goodbyes began. The lads from Brighton had now also got flights to go home and the others were also making plans for their journeys back to England. On our departure day we travelled to the airport with the two girls and their tickets. They came into the airport to check us in with their passports, then handed us their tickets, we paid them our money, the deal was done and we were away. As easy as that. I still get palpitations at the thought of it now; we really had no idea just how dangerous it was, but it did seem to be what everybody else was doing back then, so we just went with it. Of course, we didn't mention any of this to my parents, who were coming to the airport to pick us up in England as we didn't think there was any point worrying them unnecessarily.

We were sad to be leaving our little family in Magaluf but excited to be going home to our families and friends back in England. All went fine at the airport in Majorca; a little late setting off, but very smooth regarding tickets. Both Stacey and I had a good few brandies; this was an essential process for me, to actually get me on to a plane. My fear of flying wasn't getting any better, but I wasn't going to let that stop me from travelling. I'd flown enough times by now with Stacey that she knew exactly how many brandy and cokes it would take to get me up the airplane steps.

The flight home went well with no problems. It wasn't until we came to reclaim our bags back at the airport in England that things suddenly started to change. I suppose we'd been in the sun for a full two months now, and sunbathing had been our main job. Stacey was extremely brown to say the least, with her olive skin; even I, with my blue/white complexion, had gained quite a lot of colour. Our hair was very bleached-blonde and all the luggage we owned was in a rucksack. I'm sure you're getting the picture. We looked like we'd been travelling for a long time!

Well, one minute Stacey was admiring the lovely little dog that had come out to see us both – it did seem to really like us, especially Stacey and her rucksack. I was just calling it over to come and see me for a stroke when all of a sudden we were both being led very briskly out of the customs area to a private room. Stacey seemed to be going in one direction whilst I was going in the other. It was at this point that alarm bells started ringing. What on earth was going on?

All was soon to be revealed: it turned out that one of the travellers who had been living in our apartment with us had been borrowing Stacey's cut-off dungarees to go to work in. This, of course, we knew about, but what we didn't realise was that he'd been keeping his stash of 'weed' in the top pocket of them. Would you believe that Stacey almost forgot them! It wasn't till we'd left the apartment for the airport that she remembered and went running back in for them. Perhaps this would have been one of the rare times when her amazing ability to lose or forget things would have been to our advantage! Our roommate hadn't been silly enough to leave any of his supplies in there, but there was, unbeknown to us, traces of it in her dungarees pocket. This was enough evidence for the clever sniffer dogs to find, and, of course, they needed to be sure that we didn't have any more with us, or on us. So what followed next was a full strip-search, and I mean full. In-between toes, inside ears, up nostrils, and would you believe people must try get though customs with it in their mouths? Because when they told me to bend over and part my cheeks, there was a little confusion. When I put my hands to my mouth and bent over, pulling my cheeks apart, I was thinking, well they're not going to be able to see in my mouth when I'm bent over.

'What do you want me to do that for?'

'Wrong cheeks' came the stern reply.

I was mortified. Surely they didn't mean those cheeks? Unfortunately for me they did, and this was one of those life situations where you think to yourself, I'm dreaming this, any minute now I'm going to wake up. But I'm afraid I didn't and over the next fifteen minutes my life flashed before me as I knew that even if I didn't get arrested here and now and even if I did make it through to the other side of customs, my parents were probably going to kill me anyway. At this point I could feel myself wanting to cry, and I probably would have done had I not heard Stacey in the other room saying, 'They don't put it there, do they!?'

Of course, they found nothing and as they were leading me out of my room Stacey was just coming out of hers. She looked over at me, it was a look I'd never seen before: her tan had completely gone! We were now free to go, but to be honest I just wanted to stay there, as by now my parents had been waiting for a least three hours. They would have seen our plane land, and what if they'd gone to enquire whether we were on the flight? We weren't even travelling under our own names. I knew that by now they would have been panicking, wondering where an earth we'd got to and if we were okay. I was far more scared of them than any police or security man. How on earth could we tell them what had just happened? We headed straight for the toilets.

Amazingly, Stacey and I came up with a very quick plan. We decided to tell them that our bags had been searched because we had our hairdressing equipment (including powder bleach) in them, that and the fact that we'd been away for so long had made them suspicious as to our intentions. Pretty quick thinking, especially after what we'd just been through.

Well, it must have worked as they were just so relieved to see us, after such a long delay, and they didn't ask too many questions. I could see my dad towering above everyone else, looking very worried, staring at the arrivals board.

'Dad! Dad! We're here!' I shouted to him as soon as the arrivals doors opened.

Rushing over to him and Mum, Stacey and I nearly knocked them both over, we were so pleased to see them. Mum was already crying, and soon we all joined in. They were beginning to wonder if we'd missed our flight; had we been much longer they were going to enquire at the desk. We were extremely relieved they hadn't, as we didn't want that can of worms opening. It was so good to see them; I think they'd missed us a lot. Dad always loved to listen to the stories from our holidays; he'd sit for hours listening and chuckling at what we'd been up to, so there was plenty for him to catch up on.

'We've loved getting all your letters, can't wait to see all the photos. Then we can put faces to all your friends' names,' he said in the car on the way home.

Stacey and I both glanced over at each other, thinking the same – that we didn't want to see one of those friends' faces for quite some time. We talked Mum and Dad to death all the way home in the car, hardly stopping for breath, telling them all – well nearly all – that had happened to us over the last two months.

Coming back home took a bit of settling in. Getting up for work every morning was hard, but after a while it was nice to have money to spend, have my own bar of soap, and I hadn't realised just how much I'd missed my own bed. We both enjoyed home-cooked food – not a sign of any eggs, beans or bread anywhere. It was so lovely to see all our friends again; although we'd enjoyed writing to and receiving letters from them all, we'd missed them a lot. Anybody would have thought we'd been away for years. There was just so much for us to catch up on. Stacey and I still spent a lot of time together when we got back. A few months after the trip, one evening whilst Stacey and I were out in town, she got chatting to a friend of mine, Jason. As they seemed to be getting on quite well, I ended up chatting to his mate, Gary.

This was the start to a new chapter, as they were best friends and we were best friends. Well, maybe it was meant to be . . .

3

Didn't see that coming

It was October 1992 and a day both Stacey and I will never forget.

That day, Stacey had the heartbreaking job of moving her dad, Peter, into a nursing home. He was only fifty-nine. How unbelievably sad. He had been suffering now for nine years with Parkinson's disease; he'd deteriorated so much that the time had finally come where he now needed twenty-four hour care. Stacey's mum, Pam, was also struggling with her health as she'd had ME for years, but recently with the stress and worry about Peter she too was much worse. In fact, she was probably the worst I'd ever seen her. Although Stacey had tried so hard to keep everything going at home for them all, I guess we knew this day would eventually come. On this particular morning Pam couldn't even get out of bed – she was just too weak – so Stacey had rung to ask me if I could help her with today as she knew it was going to be tough.

'Yes of course I can, no problem. All I have to do today is ring the doctor between four and five, so don't let me forget.' I'd had a silly bladder infection for quite some time, couldn't seem to get rid of it, so I was hoping the test results would say I didn't need any more antibiotics.

We arrived at the nursing home in good time and got Peter settled into his room. As we started to unpack some of his things and put them into the drawers it was hard to believe that this was happening to Stacey and her family. It was a lovely place and Peter's room was nice. The staff were very kind, coming in and out, bringing lunch and chatting away to us all, but it was still the hardest thing for Stacey. At just twenty-three she'd already been through so much. I felt so helpless and guilty that my parents were both well.

The day flew by and when I checked the clock on Peter's wall, it was almost five.

'Stacey, I've forgotten to ring the doctors.'

'Oh no, I forgot all about that. I'll ask the nurse if there's a phone you can use.'

The nurse led me downstairs to an empty office. It was long before the days of mobile phones. Thinking that the doctors may already have closed, I was relieved when the receptionist answered. She put me straight through to the doctor.

'Yes, hello, Joanne. I have some good news for you, and some other news. Your bladder infection has cleared up fine, and ... and you're pregnant.'

Oh my god. I'm what? I was speechless. Pregnant? I couldn't possibly be! Could I? Well, apparently I was. Oh my god.

'Are you okay, Joanne?' asked the doctor.

How can I tell Stacey this? Hell, should I even tell her today? She's got enough going on. Pregnant? Me? No. I think they must have my results mixed up with someone else's. Yes, there's got to be some kind of mix-up.

'Joanne, are you still there?'

'Oh, yes, sorry, yes I'm here,' I stuttered.

'A little bit shocked, then, I presume?'

Shocked. That's an understatement. Oh no, what will Gary say? And my mum and dad? Oh, and Gary's mum and dad too? Thoughts of panic were racing through my mind. The doctor finally went after realising he wasn't going to get much sense out of me, telling me to ring and make an appointment with the midwife.

What was going on? I stayed in the office downstairs, stunned, for about twenty minutes, feeling quite sick and shaking slightly. Knowing that I had to go back soon otherwise Stacey would be coming to look for me, I eventually went back up to Peter's room, where Stacey was helping him with his cup of tea. She looked over at me. I didn't need to say anything to her. I must have been as white as a ghost by now because she knew something was wrong.

'Are you okay?' she asked, looking very concerned.

'My bladder's fine, yes thanks, but apparently I'm ... pregnant.'

Poor Peter ended up with most of his cup of tea down himself as he shouted at us in his strong Glaswegian accent, 'What's bloody going on?!'

'You're not! You can't be! How? Shit, you'd better sit down.'

We both stared at each other for a good few minutes and as Stacey sponged the tea from her dad's trousers she kept looking over and shaking her head at me. I felt like someone had just hit me over the head with a sledgehammer. I was in shock, I think. What was I going to do now? Then, after staring into space for a good while, I glanced over at Stacey. She started to smile at me. It was the first time I'd seen her smile all day.

'Well, you've really done it this time,' she said as her smile broke into laughter.

Then out of sheer shock I too burst out laughing – although I wasn't exactly sure what it was I was laughing at. Tears were trickling down our faces and I looked across at Peter, who was now also smiling and starting to giggle with us. We were all laughing quite uncontrollably when one of the nurses came back into the room.

'Well, it's good to see so many happy faces. It makes a nice change around here.'

None of us filled her in on the joke.

*

Peter was still chuckling at us when it was time to leave. It had obviously tickled him and leaving him smiling that evening certainly made things a little easier for Stacey. After saying goodbye, we made our way back to Stacey's car. We were both still in shock; the laughter had just about worn off.

'Where do you want dropping off, then?' she asked

'The moon, I think.' A bit more nervous laughter escaped. 'Well, I suppose I'd better go and see Gary.'

At this point Gary and I had only known each other for nine months. We were having a great time – obviously! Gary was a fire-fighter at the station just down the road from where he lived. He owned a little house that he'd been living in for about eighteen months. I was still living above the hair salon; my mum and dad had now retired from the business and had moved out to the country-side. So my brother Steven, who was now studying at university, had moved back in. We each had our own room and we were renting the spare room to a friend of ours, Philip. He was a guitarist and Steven being a drummer meant that there was always music and noise around the place. They would often rehearse at our house with the rest of their band members, which I loved. In fact, both their bands became quite famous around Yorkshire and I always enjoyed hearing the songs before anyone else did. All in all, it was a very busy, lively place. With the shop opening six days a week, friends would always drop in. Everyone met there before nights out, and the parties we had were the best. We were very happy there, and I definitely had no plans to change things.

As only a true friend would, Stacey agreed to come in with me to tell Gary. He was as chilled as ever when we arrived; however, I was feeling rather sick by now. He seemed pleased to see his unexpected visitors and perhaps a little confused. •

'So you were just passing and thought you'd call in?' he said as he handed me a cup of tea.

'Yes,' I said nervously.

Stacey at this point was trying to get her whole head into the biscuit barrel, and most likely hoping that the ground would soon swallow her up.

'I just wondered what you were doing next August,' I blurted out. Well, it was the best I could come up with.

'August ... August ... not sure. Why? Do you want to go on holiday?'

Oh well, here goes ...

'No, no I was thinking, if well, err, maybe you might like to come to the maternity ward with me?'

His smile froze for a few seconds, and then I could almost see his brain digest what I'd just said. Everyone was completely silent; I hadn't dared look over at Stacey – I think she'd stopped breathing at this point.

'What? Why? You don't mean ... You're not pregnant? Are you?'

4

Growing my own baby

Packing up all my things was hard. I was feeling so sick, and although I was very excited at the prospect of moving in with Gary I was reluctant to leave my life behind at the salon. It really was all I'd ever known – well, apart from my two months in Magaluf of course. Having now broken the news to the rest of the world and surviving telling both sets of parents, it suddenly felt all very real.

It was now December and looking pretty much like the doctors were right after all, certainly from the way I was feeling and looking, and so according to their records I was about sixteen weeks into my pregnancy. After a lot of talking, Gary and I had decided I would move into his house with him. It made perfect sense really. We were very lucky that he already had a house; it was quite a way from where I'd been living, but it was plenty big enough and the spare room would be perfect for the new baby.

As the months passed by, I got fatter and fatter but the sickness did seem to wear off, and that was a huge bonus. Lying in the bath most evenings I would watch the baby's arms and legs moving about, which was very weird, almost alien-like. No doubt about it, I was definitely pregnant.

All went pretty calmly throughout the pregnancy. We were advised to go along to some of the antenatal classes by the doctor. We felt a bit nervous on our first visit, but everyone seemed very nice there, although I couldn't help but notice that they were all quite a bit older than Gary and I. We talked about a birthing plan, where you can actually decide how you want to have your baby – lying down, sitting up, or even in a special bath! I liked the sound of the bath: seemed calming and relaxed, very idyllic. Pain relief was also talked about: gas and air, TENS machines, epidural and pethidine. So you could do the whole thing without any pain at all? Now, that sounded good to me.

'Oh, I'll refuse any pain relief. I want to do it all natural,' I overheard the lady at the side of me say.

'Really, why?' I said, totally confused. She looked at me like I'd just dropped out of the sky.

'Well, of course you don't want any pain relief. You want to be able to know what's going on and feel your baby coming out.'

I must have looked confused, as she promptly stopped talking.

Did I want to feel it? Not sure if I did, really. Why would you want to be in pain? I thought to myself. But still, each to their own, I suppose. We then got shown how to do some controlled breathing, which is what you need to be doing in-between contractions. It's to help you focus and to stop you from pushing when it's too soon to push. Looks and sounds strange when people are doing it, rather like a dog panting away. I did feel a bit silly trying that, to be honest, and poor Gary didn't know where to look. I think most of the men in there would have just been better off going to the pub and leaving the women to it. They were all pretty embarrassed, except for one guy – he was getting well into it, breathing in and out very deeply, making a lot of noise ... anybody would have thought he was having the baby. We were supposed to be doing this with our eyes shut, but I couldn't resist peeking at him, and I did notice plenty of the other people in the class looking at him too – although as he did have his eyes closed, this wasn't much of a problem. It did just seem like very strange behaviour to me. Panting like a dog didn't really appeal to me, or Gary for that matter, thank goodness. Then the teacher started talking about breastfeeding.

'Breast is best,' she kept saying. 'Yes, it's the most natural thing in the world, ladies!'

I wasn't too sure about that either. I couldn't really imagine being comfortable getting my boobs out every few hours. Although it's supposed to be much better for the baby, I would just have to see how I felt once it was born. This still all felt a little strange to say, as it still hadn't quite sunk in at this point. Was I really going to have a baby?

After a few more monthly visits to listen to the 'breast is best' brigade and the heavy-breathing father-to-be, we were nearly there. August had finally arrived, which was just as well, as by now I was nearly as wide as I was tall! Everyone was getting excited. They couldn't wait to see what the baby was going to be like.

'Oh, it'll be so laid back, just like you and Gary are' seemed to be the general opinion with all our friends.

As the baby's due date passed, I'd been having a few pains here and there. Finding myself quite uncomfortable one afternoon and taking on board what I'd been told at my classes, I got into the bath to see if that would ease the pains. Gary spent about two hours juggling to keep me entertained. Him and a few of his friends at work had started juggling just a few months before and he was becoming quite good at it.

'I hope you're still here when it gets dark, then I can get my new luminous juggling balls out and show you them,' he laughed.

I was kind of hoping it would all be over by the time it got dark. The hours went by and Gary did get his wish: I was still there after dark. So out came the next pair of balls! They were very luminous. It looked quite impressive and at first it was entertaining, but as time went on and I was becoming more tired and uncomfortable, it suddenly didn't seem that interesting anymore.

'Just keeping your mind off things, love,' he kept saying. 'At this rate, I'll be brilliant at this soon. I'll be able to join the circus.'

By this point I was beginning to wish he'd just go and join a circus, a clear indication that my sense of humour was slowly disappearing. Unfortunately, this all turned out to be a false labour! The pains then disappeared without a trace, leaving me very tired and fed up. We'd been awake most of the night so I took myself off to bed to try and get some rest and maybe find my sense of humour again.

That evening Gary was due to go on to nights, so rather than be on my own I'd asked my brother Steven to come and stay, just in case something happened. I was kind of hoping that it wouldn't: Steven wasn't one for coping with poorly people and certainly didn't like hospitals. In fact, I'm almost certain that had anything started that night, he would have just freaked out. Luckily for him, all was very quiet that evening.

5

Patience is a virtue

The pains began again just after Steven left that next morning. Gary returned home from nights and took me straight to the maternity ward. I was examined, and was only two centimetres dilated. Apparently, you need to be at least three to be in true labour, so they sent me home.

I cried all the way home in the car. I was getting really fed up now, wondering if this baby was ever going to come out. Having just nicely got in the door at home, the pains returned once more, only this time they really were strong.

'Come on, we'll go back,' Gary said.

'No, I daren't. What if they stop again? I'll feel stupid,' was my teary reply. I didn't want to appear pathetic before we'd even got started.

Well, I tried to be brave. We sat watching Fawlty Towers videos for about five hours, just trying to keep my mind off things. But as the day went on even Basil Fawlty wasn't making me laugh anymore. So, it was then back in the car, on our way once more to the hospital. Three centimetres this time – thank goodness, I could stay. A nervous excitement went through me. This is it, then – we're off, I'm going to have a baby. As the hours went by, with each examination I was hoping for progress, but each time I remained the same. 'No, sorry, Joanne you're still at three centimetres,' the midwives kept telling me.

I was working my way nicely through all the different pain reliefs. The gas and air helped a bit, but after quite some time on that, I was starting to feel sick so I had to stop with it, because throwing up in-between contractions was really no fun and not at all helpful.

Twelve hours into my labour it was decided they'd put me an epidural in, so I could get some sleep, ready for labour. I was already exhausted; I didn't sleep much but I did shut my eyes and rest. It was so nice not to be feeling the contractions and be out of pain for a while. The midwife, Sarah, was a star; she was very near to finishing her training – only one more delivery and she would have completed her forty births, which she needed to do to be fully qualified.

'Come on, Joanne, my shift finishes in six hours. I need you to have your baby before then.'

Sadly, she had to go home, and still no baby. As she was leaving, though, she did promise that she'd come to see me and the baby the next day when she came back into work. The new midwife was great too, even though she came in with a team of students following her.

'Do you mind if they come in and have a look, Joanne?'

'Yes, bring them in. They all have to learn,' I remember saying to her; I was past caring now and all I wanted to do was just go home and forget the whole thing. There were now four students, two midwives and two doctors in the room with us and I was beginning to get just a little bit scared. Poor Gary looked dreadful but still, I'm sure, slightly better than me ... and he had, at last, stopped juggling! We'd now been going for about thirty hours and as a couple more midwives arrived to examine me I could feel myself becoming quite panicky. I didn't know what was going on anymore. Why were all these people so interested in me?

'Okay, Joanne, you're just about ten centimetres now, but the baby is lying sideways, so we need you to push when you have a contraction. With your epidural, you won't be able to feel the contractions, but we'll tell you when you're having one. This should help baby to turn as it comes down the birth canal.'

So I pushed, and I pushed, and I pushed! For a good few hours or so. Still nothing. Everyone seemed confused. They were all scratching their heads when who should come in but Sarah, back on shift.

'Hey, Joanne. I can't believe you're still here.' It was lovely to see her smiling face – although I did suddenly have the urge to cry, as I couldn't believe I was still here either. That meant another twelve hours had gone by. None of those books I'd read had mentioned this.

'Well at least I can still be your fortieth delivery!' I said to her. She just smiled at me.

After another three doctors had been in to see me, it was decided that I would go into theatre. They were going to try the rotating forceps first and hoped this would work, but if not they were going to have to push baby back up the birth canal and do an emergency caesarean!

Wow really, is that possible? I started to think to myself. Then I quickly dismissed the thoughts I was having. I really had changed my mind now. I just wanted to go home, forget the whole thing. Maybe this was all a dream and I was going to wake up soon. My epidural was topped up again, and I was whizzed down to theatre. Gary had disappeared – I wasn't sure where – and Sarah was holding my hand. As they were putting up the screen, the room was quickly filling with people, all dressed in blue with blue masks on. All I could hear was my heart beating very loud in my head and I was shaking, and I thought I wanted to be sick again. Then one of the doctors came to the top of the bed and held my other hand. I was just thinking how lovely and blue his eyes were above his mask.

'How you doing, love?'

It wasn't till he spoke that I realised it was Gary, all dressed in blue. Another tear trickled down my cheek. Was I going to die? What about the baby? The poor little thing has been trapped in there trying to get out for days. Is it going to be all right?

Rotating forceps aren't the smallest of tools; thankfully I couldn't quite see them over the screen, but I could see the young doctor, who was trying really hard to get to the baby. I knew she was struggling; I could only see her eyes above her mask, but that was enough. There was panic in them, and in my heart I just knew that she wasn't going to be able to get to the baby with the forceps. Despite there being so many people, the room was silent and you could feel the tension.

This is it, then. The end. We're both going to die here. I was staring at Gary hoping he was going to tell me it was all going to be okay. He just kept squeezing my hand, but there was nothing he could say as he had no idea what was going on either. Then, just at this point, when I was going to remind Gary that I wanted Michael Jackson's *The Way You Make Me Feel* playing at my funeral, this gorgeous-looking guy popped his head round the door. Now, under normal circumstance I would have been alarmed as I wasn't perhaps looking my best or in the best position for meeting new people – especially one that looked like this – but it turned out that he was the head doctor who had been called. As he took a look around the room, I think he could feel the tension, which instantly told him the answer to his question.

'I'll get scrubbed up,' he announced.

He obviously did and then re-appeared, as if by magic like Mr Benn, in his blues. Now, it could have been the drugs, but I'm sure I saw little halo above his head. He came to the top end of the bed to talk to me.

'My name's Doctor Stuart, Joanne, and I'm going to have a go at getting your baby out for you.'

I wasn't overly bothered who he was. He could have been Tom Cruise for all I cared at this point as long as he knew what he was doing. Well, it turns out he did. There was a good deal of pulling and pushing, but within ten minutes he'd done it, he'd got the baby out and there was a cheer from around the room.

I looked at Gary. We were both waiting to hear that little cry, which soon came, and then that little cry turned into a big cry. We couldn't believe it – at last it was all over. So after fifty-six hours of labour, on Thursday 5th August at 3.58pm, Abbie Rose finally made an appearance.

6

Who is that monster?

At about six that evening, after I'd had one or two stitches and a few pints of blood, Abbie and I were wheeled back up to the ward. Gary looked exhausted; thank goodness I couldn't see what I looked like. There were about fifteen concerned family members and friends all waiting for us as we came down the corridor towards the ward. Nobody had heard anything from us since we'd gone in and I think by then everyone was very relieved to see us all. A good few tears were shed when people saw little Abbie: she was so tiny and beautiful, all wrapped up in her pink blanket. Then, as people glanced over at me they seemed a little disturbed. Now, I've never been blessed with a great deal of colour in my cheeks, but over the last few days any colour I did have had been completely drained from me. The red and white checked gingham nightgown they'd given me for theatre really did do very little to flatter my complexion.

My once quite large eyes were just peeking through the now extremely heavy lids, which were slowly taking over my whole face. As for the rest of my body ... well, that was mostly in tatters. In fact, I would say the television series *The Walking Dead* springs to mind.

Abbie was the first baby to be born out of our group of friends, so you can imagine how excited everyone was, all wanting a cuddle and a photograph with her. She had plenty of bruises on her little head from the traumatic delivery she'd been through, but of course she was still the cutest thing we'd ever seen.

After visiting time was over, Gary had to go home. I just sat staring at Abbie. Look at what we've made ... wow, it's a real person ... but what on earth do we do with it now?

The lady in the next bed, Carol, had just had her third baby. She was a real professional and I did seem to keep asking her lots of questions. I'm sure she was thrilled to have me in the next bed, especially as the night went on, because Abbie cried for most of it. She certainly did seem to have a great pair of lungs on her. I was finding it rather difficult getting in and out of bed and as Abbie seemed to be waking up every two to three hours, I was up and down most of the night. They'd given me a rubber ring to help with the pain when sitting down. It did help a little but it wasn't the easiest thing to get on or off of, especially with a baby in your arms. It was a long night. I was exhausted and all I really wanted to do, more than anything, was just go to sleep.

One of the things that was never mentioned to me, by anybody, not even the 'breast is best' brigade, was piles. Now then, if you're laughing at that word, 'piles', you've obviously never had the pleasure of them. On the other hand, if you're cringing then I'm guessing you probably have. One or two are very uncomfortable, but the amount I had from my ten hours of unsuccessful pushing ... 'agony' is the only word to explain them. Understandably, I never saw them myself, and definitely didn't want to. I knew that they must have been pretty horrific from the expression on the faces of the poor doctors that had the delightful job of examining them. They made any kind of movement difficult; even coughing and laughing were excruciatingly painful!

With this in mind, the last thing you want to be doing when you have piles is to be constantly getting in and out of bed. Attempting to sit down isn't easy, and going to the toilet – well, I won't even go there. However, just to give you an idea of how many there were, our five-day stay in hospital after Abbie's birth was so that I could have regular treatments to reduce them in size! Add this to the amount of stitches I'd had, after the very clever rotating forceps, and I think you're getting the picture. Uncomfortable doesn't even touch it.

Looking back, I'm guessing at this stage that I wasn't in a very good place at all, mentally or physically. The midwife wasn't aware of my traumatic night, or indeed the few days before it, when she asked me how the breastfeeding was going. I wasn't very happy doing it at all. Apart from it being almost impossible to sit down anywhere, never mind get comfortable, I really wasn't even sure that I was doing it right. When it was getting near to visiting time, I could feel myself becoming more and more worked up, panicking in case she needed feeding whilst everyone was here. It would be so embarrassing, and clear to them all that I didn't have a clue what I was doing.

'How's the breastfeeding going, Joanne?' said the cheery midwife when she flew in the next morning.

'Oh, it's not really going at all. I'm not sure what I'm doing wrong, but Abbie's been awake most of the night again, so I don't think I can be doing it right.'

'Nonsense. There's no such thing as doing it wrong, Joanne. It's the most natural thing in the world. Breast is best.'

'You do it, then, if you think it's so easy!' is what I really wanted to say to her as it didn't feel at all natural to me and I wasn't too sure Abbie was enjoying it either. At this point she woke up, again.

'Perfect timing. I can watch what you're doing before I go. I'll pass her over to you, and we'll get her latched on.'

Oh, yes, great, let's get her latched on then, to what's left of my nipples! I didn't think it was possible for my nipples to get any more painful than they already were, but the midwife didn't seem to be too bothered about that. No, nothing was going to stop her on her 'breast is best' mission, and before I could say another word she was trying to attach Abbie to my burning nipple. Abbie thrashed about furiously, which wasn't helping much, and I was in agony.

'There you go, you're doing great!' she shouted as she scurried away.

Don't go, please don't leave me, I was thinking as a tear escaped and trickled down my chin, but it was too late – she was gone, away to the next poor victim.

Doing great? Well, how come I feel so dreadful then? Apart from the fact that I can't sit down, get in or out of bed and haven't been to sleep for four days I've now got this small person swinging on my extremely sore nipple. She's no idea what she's doing, and I've no idea what I'm doing. I just want somebody to get me a bottle of milk for her. Someone else can feed her then – anybody, I don't care who – then perhaps I could just go to sleep.

The next night was much the same as the night before.

I couldn't help but notice that I was the only one who was up all night. The other babies did wake up, of course, but they didn't make too much fuss about it and no way were they anywhere near as loud as Abbie. They were fed and changed in what seemed like no time at all. Then straight back off to sleep. As were their mums.

A very strange thing happened that next morning. I'd eventually managed to fall asleep on my back after trying, quite unsuccessfully, to feed Abbie for what felt like most of the night. I was woken up by pins and needles in both arms and was slightly panicked by this, remembering hearing somebody at some point saying that pins and needles down your arm was one of the first signs of a heart attack. Then I realised even though I was lying down I couldn't quite see over my chest. It was huge! I tried to sit up, but with both arms now completely numb it was impossible. I patiently waited there, helpless, until the feeling returned to my arms, praying that Abbie didn't start to cry. Then, as quickly as I could, I managed to sit up. My chest didn't move at all. It was completely solid.

'Carol! Carol! What's happened to me?' I shouted over.

'Ah, you're fine, Joanne. Your milk's coming in, love, that's all.'

That's all? What an earth was I going to do with these? Through the night my chest had grown from an extremely small 34B to at least a 34DD. They were massive. It felt like they'd been filled with lead and they were completely solid, and very painful.

'As soon as she starts to feed you'll feel better, Joanne,' Carol informed me.

Okay, great, just need her to wake up now, and that shouldn't be long then. From the short time I've known her, I've already learnt that waking up regularly is something she's mastered.

Four hours later and Abbie was still sleeping. I didn't think my chest could expand any more. I was beginning to worry that perhaps there was something wrong with her as she'd never slept for this long before. Then, just in the nick of time, only moments before my chest exploded all over the ward and after a marathon of five hours asleep, Abbie finally woke up. No sooner had she opened her eyes than an enormous breast was wavering in front of her face. Getting her latched on wasn't the easiest, as we still had no clue between us what we were doing, but eventually – after some coughing, spluttering and a few tears, from us both – we finally managed it, she was latched on. At last I could feel my chest starting to deflate, and this was a great relief for me. Abbie looked more shocked than relieved, because with the speed the milk was coming out at she had to keep stopping to catch her breath. Of course, the milk didn't stop when she did, though; no, it just kept on coming. It was everywhere, and by the time she'd finished we were both absolutely soaked. As I rummaged around in my hospital bag for a clean nightie, I came across a packet of breast pads. Aha, now I knew what these were for.

On the morning of 8th August after another exhausting night in and out of bed far too many times, I suddenly remembered it was my birthday. I hadn't mentioned it to anyone else on the ward, as Carol had now gone home and I hadn't really spoken to any of the new ladies that much yet. Abbie was asleep, so I thought it was a good time to go and have a wash and get myself sorted for the day. The toilet experience was as joyful as ever: there was still much more of my insides on the outside, as it were. Having made the unwise decision to glance in the mirror as I went past it only confirmed my growing fear: my eye sockets were no longer there. They'd completely disappeared, there was a flap of skin on each side where they once had been, and my eyes looked half the size I remembered them to be. I was pale green/white in colour, and my hair, well, big is the best way to describe it – big and out of control! Abbie was three days old today and I was twenty-five. That means when she's twenty-five I'll be fifty! Now, that's a jolly thought. In fact, the more I tried to have jolly thoughts the more I seemed to be spiralling downhill to despair. Then suddenly I remembered: this was something I'd been told about. Three to five days after having a baby you can get what they call the baby blues. I'd read all about this, but I hadn't taken much notice of it; I actually thought that it was all a load of rubbish. Well, how wrong was I! For the next twenty-four hours at least, I think all I did was cry. Every time someone so much as looked at me I'd just well up. Those poor people that came to see me with cards and things for my birthday. Hysterical is the best way to describe my behaviour. How pathetic. But I just couldn't stop crying. Self-pity had set in and it would appear that there was absolutely nothing I could do about it.

The evening trip to the bathroom was no better, as a day full of crying certainly hadn't enhanced my looks in any way. Why I took a second look in the mirror that day I'll never know, as I really didn't recognise this monster who was staring back at me in the reflection. As if that wasn't bad enough, I still couldn't poo! That was a bit of a worry because they'd told me that until I'd managed to go to the toilet they couldn't let me go home. So this was it, then – I was going to have to stay here, probably forever, as there was no way I could imagine being able to push, ever again. All I wanted to do was go home – at least I thought I did, but I don't think I was quite sure what I wanted to do anymore, or even which home I want to go to. I just wanted my mum.

Yes, my mum will know what to do. She loves babies and I'm her baby so why can't she come and look after me?

I couldn't possibly lie on my front now as my boobs were far too big and my nipples were raw. I'd been so looking forward to lying on my front again, having not been able to do so throughout my pregnancy. 'Breast is best.' I still wasn't so sure about that myself and I couldn't get that woman's voice out of my head.

By now I'd got pretty good at positioning myself on the bed with the rubber ring that they had given me, and several cushions. My main problem was getting in and out of bed: it just seemed so high. Unbeknown to me, the bed had been on the highest setting and it wasn't until I was leaving hospital to go home that the midwife informed me of this.

'How have you managed with this bed, Joanne? It's on the highest setting.' Then she proceeded to pump the handle on the side to show me how it went up and down.

I just presumed it was so high because I'm only four foot eleven inches. So I never questioned anyone about this super-high bed. Instead I'd managed to master a technique to get in and out: I would put Abbie under my left arm, then, taking a small run towards the bed, I would kind of pole-vault on to it with her, always making sure I landed on my right side as not to squash her, and of course never landing on my bottom as that would've been torture. In fact, after a few days of training using this technique, I was actually becoming rather good at it.

So, then at last, five days after Abbie had been born, after things had been stitched, shrunk and put back into place and with just a little white lie about going to the toilet, we were finally allowed to come home, safe in the knowledge that my birthing plan definitely hadn't come off!

7

Sleep

Over the next few weeks Abbie's sleeping habits soon became apparent: she didn't have any!

It seemed sleep was very low down on her priority list, but up at the top, very definitely in first place, was crying. I remember clearly the first night when Abbie and I arrived home from hospital. Gary was so excited; he was hanging of the end of the bed looking at her, fast asleep in the little Moses basket.

'When will she wake up?' he asked excitedly.

'Oh, soon, very soon,' I said with a smile.

As Abbie was the firstborn, many of our friends would very kindly offer to babysit. This was usually the last time we saw them. You see, from about 6pm in the evening until 1am she was probably at her worst. Our evening routine soon became myself and Gary taking it in turns to pace up and down the living room to keep her constantly on the move as this seemed to be the only thing that would stop her from crying.

When she did eventually drop off to sleep, we'd ever so gently put her down. If we were lucky, she might sleep for five minutes or so before we heard that all too familiar sound of her 'delicate' little cry. It was as if the more we jogged her around, the more she liked it, because as soon as she was still for any amount of time, she'd be back awake, seemingly furious that we'd dared to put her down in the first place. Sharing this ritual was pretty tiring in itself, especially as when she did finally go to sleep at around 1am, it was never for more than three hours. Then all too soon she'd be wide awake, crying once more and ready for another feed and a nappy change.

Now I'd seen plenty of babies come in our salon at work. Their mums had brought them in with them when they'd come for their hair appointments. They were usually all tucked up in the little car seats and they'd sleep there for quite some time, happily, whilst their mums relaxed and had their hair done. Then, as they were waking up, they would slowly start to come round with a gentle noise, and then this little gentle sound would gradually get louder and longer before they eventually started to cry. By this time, their mums would have got their bottle of milk nicely warmed through and all ready to go, calmly and with very little fuss. Well, it didn't tend to work like that with Abbie as we never got any kind of warning that she was even thinking about waking up. She could go from appearing to be fast asleep to full-on hysteria in seconds. It was as if one minute everything was fine with her and she'd be sleeping quite happily, and then all of a sudden she'd be yelling at the top of her voice and thrashing about as if she hadn't been fed for a week. It was always the same every time she woke up, day and night.

This, after only three hours' sleep, I have to say, wasn't what you wanted to hear. In fact, after a while it did start to feel like some kind of Chinese torture. I even contemplated trying to stay awake all night, as I felt this might be kinder to my body rather than letting myself nod off, only to be rudely awakened and torn from my sleep time and time again. So not surprisingly, then, we didn't have a queue of people offering to babysit, as after their first experience with Abbie they very rarely offered again. On many an occasion, we'd come home after a night out only to find the babysitters stood by the door with their coats on, looking very pale and eager to leave. Advice from people, of course, would come flooding in:

'She must have colic.'

'It'll be because of the difficult forceps delivery.'

'Is she thirsty? Try some water.'

'Is she hungry? Is she tired?'

Who knows what was going on in her little head? After a few months of this, I was beginning to wonder what was going on in mine.

As time went by I believe I did start to become a little obsessed with sleep, or rather a lack of it. Each morning, on waking, the first thing that I would do was start to count on my fingers how much sleep I'd had – usually, the one hand was all I needed. I don't think battling on with the breastfeeding was helping very much either. The health visitor just kept on saying, 'You're doing great, keep going, Joanne.' This was despite me telling her I was exhausted, delirious and possibly a little on the edge of some kind of breakdown.

What does she know? She's not even had a baby. I bet she still gets to go out with her friends on a weekend and she can eat her tea whenever she wants to, go to bed when she feels like it, get up when she wakes up, and go out of the house without thinking, will I need nappies, prams, car seats? She won't have to worry about how long she's got before the next feed or if her boobs were going to leak whilst she's out! Surely if I was 'doing great', Abbie wouldn't cry so much and would sleep more. Gary can't feed her so I have to do it all.

Each morning I would tell myself it would be the last day for breastfeeding and that I was going to try her with a bottle, but then when it came to it, I just couldn't do it. I felt so guilty, like I was letting her down and being a 'bad mother'. So this is how things continued, for quite some time.

One evening, Gary was on nights at the fire station and I was doing the usual pacing the floor with Abbie when there was a knock at the door. I suddenly thought it might be the next-door neighbours coming round to complain about the noise. Unbelievably, they hadn't been round before now, which did surprise me as the walls between our houses were so thin. Well, it was the lady from next door, and my heart sank when I saw her.

'Oh, oh, I'm so sorry about all the noise.'

'Don't worry. I've just brought this gripe water round for you to try,' she said with a smile. 'It really helped my two babies.'

Relieved that she hadn't come to moan at me about my whingeing baby, I invited her in. On coming inside she proceeded to tell me that she'd been listening to Abbie for the last few hours. Noticing that Gary's car wasn't there that evening she had thought that I might be on my own and in need of a little help. She was really kind, even trying to jiggle Abbie about for a while to give my arms a rest. Then, like everyone else that visited, she looked at me and handed her back, as if to say, I'm not sure I can shut this one up.

So, we tried to give Abbie some of the gripe water – it's supposed to help with colic. We weren't really sure whether or not she had colic, but she certainly wasn't a happy little baby, so I felt it was worth a try. I don't think pipettes were widely available then, so we had to try get some down her with a spoon. When performed on a screaming baby that was thrashing about, not an easy task. A *Krypton Factor* moment was upon us. Trisha poured some on to a teaspoon whilst I held

Abbie. We lost a few spoonfuls on our first few attempts, resulting in sticky hands for us, and Abbie ended up with it in her ears and up her nose. Then, at last, we finally managed to get some into her mouth.

Our relief was very short-lived as unfortunately the medicine had managed to go down the wrong way, causing poor Abbie to start to choke. I couldn't believe it! A huge wave of panic washed over me as I started to rub her back. Nothing. So the rubbing turned into a tap that soon became a smack. By now both Trisha and I were completely panicking. I was just about to try tipping her upside down when, at last, after what seemed like forever, I heard that familiar sound of Abbie's cry. I'd never been so pleased to hear it before – it was such a relief. My heart was beating that fast it felt like it was coming out of my chest, and I felt quite sick. That was, not surprisingly, the first and last time I tried the gripe water. Whether it would have helped her or not I'm afraid we'll never know. I wasn't going to take the risk of giving her any more, ever again. Poor Trisha felt awful and kept apologising though it, of course, wasn't her fault. She had only been trying to help.

After Trisha had gone back home I just flopped down on the sofa with a very sticky Abbie in my arms. I looked at her little face. That had frightened me so much. My hands were shaking as a tear dripped off my chin on to Abbie's forehead. She was fast asleep now ... dare I put her down? No, I might just sit here with her in my arms all night. I daren't leave her after that scare and who knows, maybe she might just stay asleep if I cuddle her. I know all the books tell you not to, but the books aren't always right.

I can't believe how much I'd taken sleeping for granted before, never giving it a thought. She'd only been here for twelve weeks and already I couldn't remember what it was like, going to bed knowing I wasn't going to get woken up until the next morning. I wondered what everyone else was up to tonight. Gosh, life seemed suddenly all so serious. All this responsibility. Where had all the fun gone? I was now starting to resemble a bullfrog as my eyelids were definitely beginning to engulf my whole face. On a breezy day, when Abbie and I ventured out with the pram, I was sure I could feel them flapping about in the wind.

Caroline, a good friend of mine, had said she was going to come over and sleep one evening whilst Gary was on nights at the fire station. I couldn't wait; I knew it would be lovely to see her and she had said she would stay up with Abbie so that I could go to bed at a 'normal' bedtime for once. I didn't actually think it was possible to get so excited about sleep, but I was ecstatic.

I had at last managed to convince myself that maybe a bottle of milk or two, in-between me feeding her, wouldn't be a bad idea – as long as I didn't have to explain myself to the scary health visitor. It meant that Gary could have a turn feeding her, something that he'd been dying to do since she'd been born. Sharing the feeds was a great help, especially the night-time ones. Not wanting to fully give up with the breastfeeding, I purchased a breast pump. This was with a view to expressing some of my milk. Not the easiest of contraptions to use. I was determined to master it, but after sitting for nearly an hour or so on numerous occasions, I never managed to express more than two ounces of milk at any one time. This, I have to say, only added to my theory: I definitely wasn't destined for breastfeeding, because if that's all she'd been getting, then it's no wonder she'd not been too happy with herself. Most likely she'd been slightly hungry, even bordering on starving.

I told them all I didn't think I was doing it right, but they wouldn't listen to me, would they? So much for 'breast is—' I wasn't even going to say it. I was sick of thinking about it. Bring on the bottle. That's milk, of course, not wine. Although that's a point – I couldn't remember the last time I'd had a glass. Felt like years.

Caroline came to sleep as promised – very brave of her as it wasn't going to be like our usual nights, where we used to just sit and drink wine and chat at our leisure. Instead it was all about keeping Abbie moving. We ate tea very quickly and both decided that wine probably wasn't a good idea.

Five hours and eighteen minutes' sleep. I can still remember it well! Thanks to Caroline. She walked the walk with Abbie, up and down the lounge, keeping her moving all the time.

'I can see a line on your carpet. Is that where you've walked up and down for the last three months?' She was right – the carpet had started to fade. 'Is this what everyone has to do with new babies?'

Well, truth was, I didn't know. I didn't think it was, actually. At this point I only had the one other friend, Sally, with a baby. Now, I'm sure on occasions she did have to do this, but certainly not every night. Again, though, when I'd spoken to people at work, they never mention pacing the floor until the early hours. In fact, I'd heard some people saying that they settle down and watch a film of an evening whilst waiting for their babies to wake up for their bedtime feed. What's all that about? Certainly wasn't how it worked at our house, I'm afraid. No, having her on the move was the only way, as soon as you stopped moving and tried to put her down, she'd wake up almost instantly!

Caroline couldn't believe it. 'I put her down so gently so she wouldn't wake up, and as soon as I walked away, she knew, the little bugger.'

Bless Caroline. I managed to get to bed at eleven that night, which was heaven, and I actually felt quite human the next day. Just as well, because I was going into work for the first time that afternoon. Only for four hours, but I was very much looking forward to it.

Going back into work and catching up with the customers and everyone else was great. Even the car journey there was so easy, just me and my handbag. I didn't have to think about the mass of other things I usually needed to take when I left the house with Abbie. I was more than happy to leave Gary in charge at home; it would be good for them both to have a day without me.

Whilst at work, though, a funny thing happened. I couldn't quite believe just what I'd done. I'm sure it had something to do with sleep deprivation and the excitement of being let out on my own for the day. Despite being a little out of practice and tuned far more into nappies, bibs and breastfeeding than hairstyling, I'd done pretty well that day and had managed to keep up with all my customers. It wasn't until I was on my last client of the day – Betty, one of the customers I'd known for a very long time. I was probably starting to tire a little at this stage and she was chattering away to me, as she always did. However, to be honest I don't think that I was really listening all that much, because she could talk for England. I must have been daydreaming quite happily to myself, because when I brought Betty up from the basin, I wrapped the towel around her head, giving her hair a good rub dry, as you do, but then, as I took the towel off her head and without even thinking about it, I just let out a very loud shout:

'Boo!'

I just blurted it out, from nowhere. I looked around to see where the shout had come from. It took me a good few seconds to work out why everyone in the salon was looking and laughing at me. Then it registered: it was me that had said it, and I didn't even realise. Was I really so tired that I didn't know what I was doing anymore? Well, I must have been. It's just a good job it was Betty, a friend of the family, and not a new customer who'd never been into the salon before. I kept having a little chuckle to myself throughout the rest of that day. Not surprisingly, it did become a bit of a joke with all the girls at work. I'd say for a good few years after that day, every so often and when I was least expecting it, as I was walking past people, minding my own business, someone would suddenly shout at me, 'Boo!'

It got me every time. I'd jump out of my skin – very amusing for all the girls at work, resulting in fits of laughter around the salon from both staff and customers.

Despite being very excited about spending some time on my own, I did seem to spend the whole day talking about Abbie, and by the time I'd finished work that day, I couldn't wait to get back home to see her. Being on my own when I'd set off that morning had seemed all very exciting, but by the end of the day, I was really starting to miss her, and I was more than ready to get back home to see how she and Daddy were getting along without me.

Words of Wisdom

As for sleep: I cannot stress enough how cross I am with myself for not appreciating one of the most natural and simple things in life. For twenty-four years and three days of my life I could have slept whenever I wanted to, for as long as I wanted. So please take it from me: make the most of it, because when that seemingly small privilege is taken away, you really are going to miss it. Lack of it can, and will, make you think and feel completely different, even do and say some very strange things.

Whilst I'm touching on the subject of taking things for granted, can I bring your attention to eyelids for a moment (the ones that sit above your eyelashes on your eye sockets – at least I think that's where they used to be). It was probably back in 1994 when I last attempted to apply eyeshadow to mine. After an unsuccessful search to find the eye contour that I was sure had once been there, it was then that I sadly realised they had now been replaced by some new, extra skin – a skin that didn't really seem to fit my face. So you might like to just take a moment, examine yours and, if they're still above rather than below your eyes, then perhaps try out some new colours with your eye makeup, have a bit of fun. As in years to come you may no longer have the opportunity, and, believe me, it's a luxury you'll miss ...

8

Your wish is my command

After three full months of beating myself up about stopping breast-feeding and worrying far too much about what the health visitor would think of me if I did, I finally made an executive decision. Enough was enough. It wasn't an easy decision but one I felt would help with my sanity. I have to say that sharing the feeds a little with Gary certainly did make things a lot easier for me. I perhaps should have done it much sooner.

There were still no signs of any of our other friends even thinking about having babies, although I'm quite sure this was due to the babysitting experiences we'd put them all through with Abbie. Looking back now, I can see I was actually feeling quite isolated at this stage. Of course, I loved Abbie very much, but so much had changed in my life in such a short space of time. I have no doubt that had she been a better sleeper things wouldn't have felt so hard. I suppose the best way I can describe it would be to say I felt like someone had clipped my wings. Everything was different: I was living away from all my close friends, who were all still doing what we'd always done together – going to work all week, with visits to the gym on an evening, then out on a weekend partying; their time was their own to do whatever they wanted. Everyone seemed to be busy getting on with their lives, going off here and there without any cares. We did go out with them from time to time, but it was always overshadowed by the thought of having to get up several times through the night, and then being up very early again the next morning.

So when I was invited to go away for the weekend to visit a friend in Windsor, I was ecstatic, realising Gary was off work that weekend. The timing couldn't have been better. It was with the girls, going from Saturday to Monday. Two nights of unbroken sleep – I couldn't wait.

Stacey and I laughed so much in the car on the way down, reminiscing about old times and some of the things that we'd got up to on our holidays abroad and nights out. My cheeks were aching from laughing before we even got there.

It was so lovely to see Poppy. We chatted and laughed all afternoon, catching up on all that had been going on. I tried not to talk too much about Abbie – I didn't want them to think that I'd become a baby bore. It felt very strange, though, being somewhere without Abbie, and every so often I had the urge to go check on her. Then I quickly remembered that there was just me to think about for the next couple of days. A flutter of excitement rushed through me.

I took absolutely ages to get ready to go out that night, just because I could. Having had a small argument with myself earlier about whether or not I should drink that night. If I didn't I could get the full benefit from my unbroken night's sleep. But should I just go for it because I could? Not taking too long to reach my decision, I went with the latter. I could sleep in the next morning – what a treat.

A great weekend was had by all. It was all fabulous, a real change. I could leave the house without doing a checklist, and I had a nice long browse in all the shops. I believe we stayed out until well after 2am. I even forgot to count how much sleep I'd had, just like the old days. We laughed loads, had a good old dance and even managed a curry. I have to say, though, that I think the best bit for me was probably the Sunday, this being because we just sat, read magazines, watched the telly and ate chocolate, a proper hangover day. I put a face mask on and sat in the bath for a good two hours. I couldn't remember when I'd last done that; my baths these days lasted all of five minutes, if I was lucky. It made me realise how I'd taken simple things for granted in the past. Stacey and Poppy must have thought I was a bit mad as I just kept repeating myself:

'This is so great. I can't tell you how nice it is.'

That afternoon we fell around laughing at one of my reading errors, something I'm well known for amongst my friends, possibly due to not listening or learning very much whilst at school! Perhaps you'd call it one of my many Joanne-isms.

It was the queen mother's birthday and there was a tribute programme on the television. When the title came up as the program was about to start, I read it out loud, in a very sarcastic voice: 'Happy birthday, ma ma!'

Stacey instantly spat her cup of tea all over, as both her and Poppy burst into fits of laughter. I was just staring at them both, wondering what an earth was wrong, hoping that they were going to start to breathe again soon.

'Its ma'am!' they both shouted simultaneously at me, once they'd started breathing again and could finally get their words out.

Realising what I'd said, and misread, soon brought me on to their level and we all sat laughing with tears streaming down our faces for a good fifteen minutes. It was possibly made even funnier by the fact that we were all extremely hungover.

It had been a fantastic weekend all round, but especially for me.

However, all that said, I'd missed the little lady. It felt like I had lost something, a bit like that feeling when you've put your cup of tea down somewhere – you know there's still some left in the cup, but you can't remember where it is. Truth be told I was very much looking forward to getting back home and seeing her that night.

Words of Wisdom

I'd say that absence definitely does make the heart grow fonder. A little break, just to re-charge your batteries, from time to time, is something I feel can be very beneficial.

As for Gary? Well I'm not so sure about him. He told me all had been fine. I know he'd spent a good deal of time at his mum's house – he wasn't daft! Although I do think he was most definitely looking forward to going back to work again, for a nice rest, if nothing else.

Oh, and I should mention to any children who may be reading this. It's not big and it's not clever not to listen at school. In this instance my reading error was quite funny, but there's been plenty of other reading errors over the years that have been rather less funny and much more on the embarrassing side.

9

Hitting the bottle

With Dad now fully retired, he often helped out with looking after Abbie on the days that I worked in the salon. It was very good of him because she still wasn't the easiest of babies to look after, as everybody had learnt by now.

As I said, Mum and Dad had moved out into the countryside and as Mum was helping out in the salon, Dad was going to have Abbie on his own at their house – he needed to be home because an engineer was coming to mend the washer. I'd carefully packed into her baby bag everything I could possibly think of that she might need for the day and off we went across the moors to Granddad's. The washing machine engineer was there when I arrived, so that was good as Dad wouldn't have to be waiting around all day for him.

'There's her bag, with everything in it. I'd best get going, I'll be back about five-thirty if that's okay,' I shouted over the noise of the washer spinning.

'Fine, love, there's no rush. We'll be "tickety-boo"' was his jolly reply.

So I set off over the moors to get to work. An extremely busy day at the salon meant that I'd not had any time at all to phone Dad to make sure all was okay. Having not heard anything from him, I just presumed that all was going well. It wasn't until I got there to pick Abbie up that evening that I realised what fun and games poor Dad had been through.

Abbie had woken up for a feed, in her usual loud manner, with no prior warning and managing to go from appearing fast asleep to being wide awake within seconds. Having gone to get her milk out of the bag, Dad had warmed it up for her in the jug of boiling water, as he always did. But when he went to test the temperature on the back of his hand before giving it to her, he noticed as he took the lid off that there wasn't a teat on the bottle. He quickly checked the other two bottles that I'd put in the bag: they, too, were missing a teat.

After searching through the bag and tipping everything out on to the table, he was horrified to find there wasn't a teat in the bag, anywhere. I'm sure at this point slight panic must have set in for Dad because, as you can probably imagine, by now Abbie was getting pretty cross and wondering just where her milk was. In fact, she was already quite inconsolable, and even though Dad was keeping her moving and jigging her about, it was doing nothing to calm her, and she was just getting louder and more distraught by the second. So the only thing Dad could think to do was to get her into her car seat, put her into his car and drive to the nearest pharmacist – this being about fifteen minutes' drive away from where he lived. Now, Dad loved looking after Abbie – he was great with her – but he was renowned for getting just a little stressed out, and he certainly didn't like hearing her cry. I can only imagine what he was going through at this point. The extremely noisy journey in the car can't have been at all nice for him, as I know for sure that she'd have only got herself more and more worked up. Other babies may well have gone quiet or even nodded off with the rocking motion of the car, even out of sheer exhaustion, but not Abbie. No. She was hardcore.

So having survived the very noisy car journey to the village, Dad then had to get this screaming baby back out of her car seat and into the chemists. She was still yelling at the top of her voice and thrashing about somewhat by this point, wondering to herself, I'm sure, why nobody had yet presented her with some milk. On entering the quiet, calm chemists, with a screaming Abbie in his arms and a nice pink baby bag over his shoulder, Dad tried to explain over all the noise that he needed another bottle, or a teat to fit the existing one. The staff must have wondered what an earth was going on. I believe one of the assistants then took Abbie from Dad to try and calm her down a little, no doubt hoping to calm Dad down in the process. Then he showed the other pharmacist the bottle to see if she could match it up with anything that they had in the shop. She had a good look around but couldn't seem to find one that would fit this bottle.

Still jigging Abbie about and trying to shut her up, the assistants were passing her from one to another when one of them shouted over her noise, 'Gosh, she's got a good pair of lungs on her, hasn't she!'

'Not half,' replied Dad.

'Is this what you're looking for?' she said, unscrewing the top off of Abbie's bottle, revealing the upside down teat that I'd put there! Oh dear, perhaps it might've been a good idea to mention that small detail to my dad. I always put them facing down into the bottle then screwed the lid on top. All that palaver that he'd had to go through, and they were there all the time. I'm thinking perhaps I wasn't his favourite person at that point ...

The assistant handed it over to him – he couldn't get the bottle in her mouth quick enough. There was instant silence. It must have been heaven, for him and everyone in there. I'm pretty sure Abbie was slightly happier too. The ladies seemed more than happy for Dad to stay there whilst she drank her milk. I don't think they'd have had the heart to ask him to go somewhere else to feed her. I feel that they could sense his relief and could see how traumatic the last hour or so had been for him.

'There's teats on these other two bottles as well,' she told him as she checked through them all.

'Great I won't have to come back in another three hours, then!' he replied with a little smile.

She soon polished that bottle off, and seemingly brought up plenty of wind – not surprising as apparently she hardly stopped for breath. The wind was just a little bit more entertainment for the staff in the chemists. The ladies then helped Dad to repack his pink baby bag, making sure he had all the other bottles in there, along with their teats. The staff had been very helpful and patient, and as Dad left he thanked them all, saying he was so sorry to have troubled them (although I do imagine that they were more than happy to have been able to help out as it had most likely livened up their otherwise quiet afternoon). So it was then back into the car and over the moors for Dad, with a somewhat happier, quieter and much calmer Abbie.

Words of Wisdom

Can we learn anything from this little mishap? Perhaps when babysitters are in short supply it's best to spend just a little time going through everything and anything that could possibly go wrong before you rush off. Luckily for me on this occasion, by the time I got back to pick her up, a good amount of time had passed and Dad had calmed down considerably. I think he was actually beginning to see the funny side of things. Just to be on the safe side, though, I did leave it a good while before I asked him to babysit again.

10

Bounce

Having Abbie on the move constantly did seem to be the way she liked it, so the pram played an important part in each day. Come rain or shine, at some point we were out with it, and this gave me a little break from keeping her on the go at home. The fresh air was good for us both, and sometimes, if I was lucky, she might even nod off to sleep, which she rarely did through the day and certainly not at home. I often popped her down into her cot to see if she needed a little nap of an afternoon. But I usually ended up, after quite some time, bringing her back downstairs again as she clearly had no intention of even closing her eyes, never mind going to sleep. So precision timing was essential with the afternoon walk: if I got it right, on occasions she'd fall asleep whilst we were out. Then it was a mad dash back home, as quickly as I could, just to try and get some jobs done, or maybe even have a little sit down with a nice cup of tea.

With this in mind, we were very excited to discover a simple yet brilliant little gadget at a friend's house, which we couldn't wait to try. Little did we know that this was to change life as we'd know it for the past six months. An ingenious invention: it was simply a clamp which fastened on to your door frame. This clamp then had some very strong elastic dangling from it, and attached to the end of the elastic was a material seat with two little holes on the bottom. These were just big enough for Abbie's legs to go through. A bouncy swing. Why on earth hadn't we thought of it before?

It was a huge success because we'd actually found something that meant that Abbie could be constantly moving, and she could do it without us. The second we'd put her into it her little face would light up and she was off. Smiling and laughing as she bounced around, she could really move in it. Side to side, up and down, round and round, it was like having a different child. It certainly gave us a rest from constantly jiggling her around. I could even move her from room to room with me, which meant that I could get a few jobs done, and I no longer had to wait for Gary to come home from work before I could start to cook tea. It made life in general much easier. Sometimes I even took her, along with her swing, into work with me. We would simply attach her to the door frame in-between the shop and the kitchen and she'd be off, more than happy there. The customers thought it was great to see her bouncing around whilst they were having their hair done. They couldn't believe how good she was in it; she really did use it to its full potential, even though she was still very tiny. Every now and then we had to grab hold of it to slow her down because we were worried that she might go crashing into the door frame, as of course at six months old she had no fear. It made Abbie much happier in general. She loved it, and so did we.

Maybe all that bouncing did have something to do with her walking long before her first birthday! She must have built up the muscles in those little legs as at only ten months old she was on her own two feet. This was perhaps helped by taking her into work with me, as Tina – one of the stylists – spent so much time encouraging Abbie to walk. Always holding on to her hands, she would patiently walk her around the salon. The more she did it, the more Abbie wanted – she never seemed to tire of it. I think Tina was more excited than me when Abbie finally took her first steps on her own. A busy little girl eager to learn right from the start, as soon as she'd mastered one thing, she quickly moved on to the next.

Words of Wisdom

So now as if by magic we had a much happier little girl. She could fulfil her need to be constantly on the move, thankfully not always assisted by us. Something so simple had made life a lot easier almost overnight. I'm afraid, though, it was already too late for the lounge carpet, as the colour had by now long gone from the middle section due to our months of pacing up and down into the early hours.

As for sleep, well, yes, there was a slight improvement, she still didn't need much of it, but it was a step – sorry, a bounce – in the right direction. Now the legs were fully working, there was suddenly so much more that she could do, and she could do it all a great deal faster.

And so the toddler is born. Now then, where shall I begin?

11

Wish you weren't here

I'm sure you've seen plenty of babies and toddlers when you've been away on holiday, out in their prams with their mums and dads on an evening. This is usually abroad, where it's warm enough to stay outside till late. The ones I'm talking about are always fast asleep, whilst their parents enjoy a well-deserved rest and a quiet drink – or perhaps, if they're very lucky, even a meal in peace. Having spent the whole day chasing around after a toddler or two, they are more than ready to have a little bit of quiet, calm time to themselves. It's a real treat to be outside, something you rarely get the chance to do in England, and the restaurants abroad seem to cater very well for this, welcoming children and babies of all ages.

So when Gary and I booked a holiday to Fuerteventura with Abbie when she was just about eighteen months old, that was exactly what we had in mind. We'd be on the beach all day with her, playing in the sand, then on an evening after her tea we would just put her into the pram, go for a little walk, she would nod off to sleep, after which we could sit down and have a few drinks in peace. It would be perfect. Or would it?

Arriving at our holiday home, which seemed to be in the middle of nowhere, the tape around the swimming pool, and the lack of water in it, caught our attention immediately. But this detail was soon to be forgotten when we went inside our apartment, which had probably last been decorated in the sixties – and judging by the smell perhaps that was when it was last cleaned. It was damp, dark and dingy. The fact that it was blowing a gale and raining outside didn't help matters much. We were extremely tired from our overnight flight and at this point we were thinking that in actual fact the weather in England in January wasn't that bad after all. I had a good few tears, probably a mixture of exhaustion and the unfortunate hotel choice, but with that out of the way, I pulled myself together and we went out to explore. This confirmed that we were definitely in the middle of nowhere.

Just across the road from our apartment, we were told, we could get a bus to a nearby beach. Our pool was to be closed for our stay, although we were allowed to use the pool in the hotel opposite. After purchasing some cleaning equipment and spraying plenty of perfume round our apartment to mask the smell slightly, things didn't look quite so grim. Gary, being ever optimistic and making the best of a bad situation, was on to it, sorting out where was probably best to go each day. It appeared our resort had very few people staying in it, and at this point there didn't seem to be a great deal going on. The sun eventually did come out; it wasn't boiling hot, but definitely warmer than it was back home. Had you been into wind surfing, you'd have been more than happy with the amazingly strong gusty winds that seemed to never let up. So we decided to take the bus into the main town and head straight for the beach. Abbie spent the entire day running up and down the beach: down towards the sea, where, on putting her toes into the water, she would scream, then run back to us. Up and down she went all afternoon; she loved it. We made sand castles, collected shells … it was perfect, just as we'd imagined it would be. With all that fresh air and running around, she was going to be so tired out tonight. I had visions of Gary and I enjoying a romantic drink or two in peace. As it turned out, Abbie had other ideas. These were based on the fact that she was going to stay awake on that holiday for as long as we did, and as we knew very well by then, determination seemed to be one of her strong points.

After the first two evenings of taking it in turns to push her up and down the promenade, we soon realised that we weren't actually spending any time with each other. One of us was sitting on their own with a drink whilst the other walked with the pram, then we'd swap. This went on for about two hours on the first night before we gave in and went back to the room. So on the second evening, after another full day on the beach in the fresh air, we took her to the disco so she could dance and run around some more.

We thought smugly to ourselves, as soon as we get her in that pram she'll be out like a light. Looking around us, all the other children were fast asleep by 9.30, even the ones that were about three or four. Abbie? Not a chance. She'd had her bedtime bottle of milk in the pram, then started shouting, 'Out! Let me out! Let me out!'

The dummy game would then begin: she would suck on it for a little while, until her eyes would start to roll and we would be thinking, yep, finally she's going off to sleep ... only, minutes later, her eyes would suddenly spring open again, the dummy would be thrown out, and it was back to square one. So we would walk some more, and then a little bit more, up and down the prom. Sure, she went a bit quiet from time to time, then, just when we thought we'd cracked it, we'd peep over at her only to find she was still wide-eyed, smiling back at us and awake! So off we all went, back to the apartment, defeated once more.

This continued throughout the rest of the fortnight's holiday. In fact, the only time that Abbie slept – and it was still only a quick nap – was late afternoon at round about 4.30, waking back up, batteries fully charged, at around 5.15.

Words of Wisdom

Unless you know the secret for getting toddlers to sleep in their prams on holiday, then your best bet, I'd say, is grandparents. Take a couple of them along on holiday with you. Or, even better, leave the kids at home with them whilst you go.

Now, I'm still not quite sure what the other parents did to get their toddlers to go off to sleep in the pram. Did it involve drugging them, maybe? Perhaps they had Velcro on their pram seats. Whatever it was, it was something we never quite mastered with Abbie. In fact, apart from that forty-five-minute nap in the afternoon, she went to bed with us at 11pm and woke up at 7am every day of that holiday.

She was certain that she wasn't going to miss out ... on a single thing!

12

Finding her feet

Having always known her own mind from a very young age, Abbie knew exactly what she wanted to wear, even from as young as eighteen months old. This often made getting her dressed quite challenging. On many an occasion, she would change my choice of clothing – usually for something extremely bright, flowery or shiny, and always things that didn't match, often summer clothes in winter and vice versa, or even a nice mixture of the them both. She was so very independent and determined, always wanting to dress herself – fastening her own buttons, zips and press studs was one of her favourite things to do. Fantastic that she wanted to learn, but this could be very testing of your patience. The fact she wouldn't allow anyone else to help her, ever, meant that this relatively simple routine could take some time and often resulted in a battle-of-wills contest between the two of us. The winner was usually determined by how much sleep we'd both had the night before. Having lived my life up until now as a relatively calm, placid person, I believe it was around about this time that I was introduced to my own temper.

On Saturdays, when I was going into work and Daddy was left in charge, I always put her clothes in a pile the night before, hoping to make things easier for him. (Also, maybe I didn't quite trust his fashion choices.) Living above the salon at this time meant that throughout the day she would often wander in to see me and everyone else, which, of course, was nice for her to be able to do, and the customers loved to see her. All would be good for a time, until she started to touch something she probably shouldn't be touching.

Taking all the rollers out of the trollies and playing with them on the floor was one of her favourite things to do. This was fine when the shop was closed, but not when we were packed out with customers on a busy Saturday. I'm not sure it would quite measure up to health and safety regulations either. As lovely as it was for her to be in the salon, inevitably there would come a time when Gary had to come and take her back into the house. Then would follow a rather loud and messy tantrum, often resulting in her being taken, or dragged, out screaming and kicking.

One particular morning does stick in my mind. Abbie had wandered in, as she often did. I glanced over at her and did a double take. What an earth was she wearing? Gary, like most men, I'm sure, wouldn't have even noticed that she'd snuck back upstairs to change after he'd dressed her earlier that morning. Now she stood there in an extremely bright pink flowery summer dress with no sleeves. She'd matched that up with some thick bottle-green woolly winter tights, bringing the whole outfit together beautifully with a pair of silver sandals. Incidentally, it was February. She would often change her whole attire completely, usually into something that she thought was far more appropriate for her day. This could be very interesting as at eighteen months old I'm sure you do have a unique dress sense, which thoughts of colour-matching and co-ordinating items don't even come into, obviously just picking the things she liked the look and feel of. Who could blame her though? That's probably the only time in your life when you can actually get away with it.

'I do it, Mummy' was, without a doubt, one of her first sentences.

Words of Wisdom

Abbie was a very strong-willed little girl right from the word go. I think it's fair to say that she had pretty much been awake for the first six months of her life. She didn't seem to need that much sleep, which was a shame, because I did. She obviously felt there was far too much to learn in life and no time to lose. Perhaps that's what all that crying had been about when she was a tiny baby – all due to her being bored, who knows? The legs were now in full swing and the vocals were coming along quite nicely too. I'm pleased to report that the crying did ease from then on. Alas, only to make way for the shouting and the tantrums.

So why is it then that we spend the first two years of their lives teaching them how to walk and talk only to then spend the rest of the time telling them to sit down and shut up?

Do we ever learn? It would appear not.

13

Say what you see

This little story took place in Blackpool. Abbie was about two-and-a-half years old and we were staying just outside the town centre so needed to catch the bus into town. This was all very exciting as it was Abbie's first time on a bus. She loved it – as soon as we got on she started running up and down, trying out all the seats before finally settling on the elevated two-seater chair in the middle area of the bus with her dad, and so I'd sat on the seat just in front of them. This had, of course, drawn plenty of attention to us from the other passengers, who were mostly smiling and finding it quite amusing. Each time the bus stopped to pick up more passengers, she found it very entertaining and was enjoying practising her counting skills.

'That's two more people on our bus now, Daddy!' she was shouting, as it drove nearer town, picking up and dropping off more people.

They all seemed quite amused by her and her running commentary, which continued throughout the journey. The two elderly ladies sat immediately in front of me kept looking back at her, smiling and laughing at Abbie's excitement at being on a bus. This is great, we were thinking, maybe we can just spend the whole holiday riding up and down on the buses to keep her entertained.

All was going fine for quite some time until a gentleman who was rather larger than the average man got on to our bus. I looked at him then quickly looked away again, hoping that Abbie wasn't staring. But what happened next assured me that she was most definitely staring at him.

As he walked passed our seats and was directly opposite us, she piped up, in a very loud voice, 'He's a big fat man, isn't he, Daddy?'

The bus went silent. I sank down into my chair, trying to make myself invisible, pretending she wasn't with me. Gary, on the other hand, had no way of escaping responsibility as he was sitting right next to her – but he'd obviously decided to pretend he didn't know who she belonged to either. The thing was, she was absolutely right – he was a huge man, and to say he wasn't would have been a great big fat lie. So what do you do in that moment of panic? Don't do what we did, because, as fairly new parents, we made the wrong decision. Don't ignore a toddler! As only seconds later, but in an even louder voice, she repeated once more, 'He's a big fat man, isn't he, Daddy?'

At this point I could feel myself wanting to laugh – not because it was funny, although I knew that one day we'd laugh about it, a lot. It was more that nervous laugh I remembered from school assemblies, when you knew you really shouldn't be laughing at all, but the more you try to stop yourself the more that urge keeps coming over you. Thing is, I could see Gary's reflection very clearly in my window as he was sat just behind me and it was dark outside, so even without looking behind I could see him squirming in his seat.

Then, as she opened her mouth to repeat herself a third time, plainly he could stand no more and he shouted over her voice, 'Come on, this is our stop!'

He scooped her up off the seat and into his arms, rather quickly, and was continuously ringing the bell as they walked down the bus towards the doors, desperately trying to keep her attention on something else. I jumped up out of my seat, still pretending that I didn't know either of them and not making eye contact with anybody else one the bus.

Although I could feel plenty of eyes on us, the two elderly ladies were pretending to look out of the window now; not surprisingly, they'd stopped smiling at Abbie. This turned out to be a good idea of Gary's, as Abbie had now joined in with him ringing the bell, believing it was a great new game. They were making quite some noise between them, but it was far too late to worry about drawing attention to ourselves. I did hope that we had a stop coming up, very soon. The bus came to a standstill. I'm not overly sure whether we'd reached a stop or if perhaps the driver couldn't stand the sound of the bell ringing continuously anymore; we jumped off regardless. The doors closed behind us and the bus drove away, and at this point we realised we actually had no idea where we were, or where we needed to be. Our relief to finally be off the bus far outweighed this small detail.

Gary was shaking his head and smiling. 'That was so embarrassing! I can't believe she said that. When I saw that guy getting on and realised she was looking at him, I was just about to put my hand over her mouth, but I didn't get it there quick enough, did I? What a nightmare!'

After several hours we eventually found where we needed to be. We had a little chat with Abbie and tried to explain to her that not all people are the same shape, size or colour. Not easy for a two-and-a-half-year-old, but we felt it had gone rather well.

That was, until two days later, when travelling on her second ever bus. She noticed a passenger who must have reminded her of something she'd watched on the television, only this time it was my turn, as I had the pleasure of sitting next to her. For some reason, Gary had sat himself on the other side of the bus.

'Mummy, that lady looks like Miss Piggy, doesn't she?'

Words of Wisdom

It's not too surprising then that these sorts of things will happen. Apart from telling you to be quicker than Gary was at attempting to shut Abbie up, I can only advise you here to maybe learn from our mistakes.

Never, never, ignore a toddler, because they won't go away, they will not shut up. In fact, they'll just get louder and louder until someone eventually answers them.

It's the luck of the draw, then, as the timing for us couldn't really have been much worse. On two buses, within two days, how very unfortunate. But as we all seem to encourage our little ones to talk as soon as they possibly can, what do we expect?

14

Sweet Caroline

I did realise quite early on that introducing a nursery rhyme cassette to a little one then inviting them to play it whilst in the car is perhaps not one of my best ideas. All appears great at first because it stops them from constantly asking 'What's this? What's that?', followed each time by 'Why?'

It gives you a bit of time to sit with your own thoughts for a change, instead of spending every car journey constantly pointing out and explaining anything and everything that moves, grows or breathes – in fact, anything remotely interesting. This is, of course, a lovely time spent with your young ones, but there is the odd time when it's the last thing you feel like doing, and that's when cassettes really come into their own. However, I must say, with hindsight, that even repeating yourself time and time again as you point out all the things you can see through the car windows has got to be better than having to listen over and over again to the same nursery rhymes. It can drive you quite mad. Especially when you've managed to buy the most annoying nursery rhyme tape that's ever been made.

You see, once you've introduced them to it, that's the only thing you'll ever be able to play in the car again. Gone are the days of having Radio 1 on and catching up on the news and weather and maybe listening to a few pop songs. You've absolutely no chance. Every now and then I would put my foot down and think, no, it's my car, I'm the adult here and I'm going to listen to the radio. This was made impossible as I could never hear it over the shouts and crying coming from the back seat.

'Mummy, Three Little Ducks, I want Three Little Ducks!' Abbie would shout constantly.

It was easier and much quieter to put it on for her and forget about the radio altogether. Friends would often ask me if I'd heard whoever's new single. Not a chance – if it didn't involve counting, colours or animals, I generally didn't know it. To make it worse, on the odd occasion that I was in the car without Abbie, I sometimes didn't even think to put the radio on. I can remember many a time arriving back home having dropped her off at nursery only to find her tape had still been playing.

However, I did have one saving grace that I managed to get away with from time to time. I told Abbie that my Neil Diamond cassette was actually one of her nursery rhyme tapes too. Sorry, Neil ... you are, of course, far more than that. I think she'd heard it played so many times she just seemed to accept it. For me this was a great relief and a welcome break from *Three Little Ducks Went Swimming One Day*. There were many other songs on the cassette, but this one certainly did seem to be her favourite, and it was the one that would be continuously going around in my head all day long.

This, I believe, is where she became a true fan of Neil, as every time we played her cassette, it was then my turn to play my nursery rhyme songs too. Just a little white lie but it seemed to work well and certainly helped to keep me sane for a good few years. When Neil announced that he was touring in 2003, I mentioned that I wanted to get tickets for my mum and me. This maybe backfired just a little, as Abbie felt that she should be coming to see him too. She knew nearly all of his songs by now and, without realising it, I think I'd turned her into a fan. It cost me another seventy pounds and, at just ten years old, she had a ticket to her first live gig. So, in November that year we set off to Sheffield arena – 'we' being myself, Mum and Abbie – to watch Neil Diamond sing some of his nursery rhymes!

I'm guessing Abbie was probably one of the youngest people in the audience that night. Having only seen pictures of Neil as a very young man on my old record covers, I think she was a little shocked when he walked out on to the stage wearing his glittery shirt.

'Who's that old man, Mummy? When's Neil Diamond coming on?'

After the initial shock of seeing a slightly older Neil, she did go on to have a great night with us. But a little bit too much fizzy pop before the concert meant that we had far too many trips to the loo, this resulting in me missing my favourite song.

Words of Wisdom

Fizzy pop and children? There's a time and a place for it, but definitely a no-no at a concert, especially when your seats are in the middle and to get out you need to ask about fifteen people to stand up. The first time is acceptable, but having had them move for your fifth visit of the night to the loo, it's understandable there's going to be a few tuts and sighs as you squeeze past them.

A big one here has got to be don't tell lies, as such a tiny white one all those years ago about Neil Diamond making a children's cassette eventually caught up with me, as lies often do. It could well be years down the line, but be sure they'll catch up with you – in this case becoming quite costly.

As for chatting to your children whilst in the car, there's nothing wrong with that. Make the most of it because there will come a day, not too far away, when the roles will be very much reversed. Then, all of a sudden, they won't want to talk to you anymore. So enjoy it while it lasts.

Children's musical cassettes and CDs might seem like a good idea, but take it from me: after a while you, too, will be driven mad by them. We gave it a miss when child number two came along. Just play the stuff you like – they'll get used to it.

15
Let's shop

You've finally got them off walking, and isn't it lovely to see them toddling around the house, pulling all your CDs and DVDs off the rack and on to the floor, pressing buttons on the telly, climbing up the furniture and generally wrecking your home? This I could usually stand for a few hours at a time until eventually I'd had enough of watching my house being 'explored'. It was then time to get them out somewhere, let them have a run and some fresh air, perhaps even take them to explore someone else's house, anywhere really would do – just out!

To have them fastened into a car seat or a pram for an hour or two is actually quite a welcome break from constantly running around the house after them, usually picking things up and putting them away only to find that when you next look round, there's no longer any visible floor space left in your lounge. Having eyes in the back of your head really would be to your advantage when dealing with a toddler. From my experiences, they generally leave a trail of devastation wherever they go.

Due to this fact, I'm all for getting them out of the house as much as possible. A nice idea, but you must take into consideration that you have to first get them into the pram or car seat. This does involve some participation on their side, and generally a toddler on the loose doesn't want to be stopped and strapped into anything. In fact, they don't want to be restrained in any way, shape or form.

Enter the 'ironing board impression', and let's face it, this is definitely one of the many vital instincts – along with breathing, sucking and crying – that babies/toddlers are all born with. They all know how to do it without being shown by anyone. But for anybody who's not familiar with this, then let me explain, and I think this trip to the supermarket with Abbie at approximately eighteen months old does exactly that ...

Abbie and I arrived at the supermarket that morning, all in good spirits even though it was raining very heavily. She was enjoying splashing through all the puddles in the car park, regardless of not having her wellies on. Consequently, we were both pretty wet through before we even got inside the store. Lifting her up to get her into the trolley seat, it soon became apparent to me that she wasn't planning a trip in the trolley around the supermarket that morning: whilst my arms were fully extended and her wet shoes were dripping all over me, Abbie had suddenly changed into what I can only describe as an ironing board. Her perfectly relaxed body had become completely rigid and she no longer bent anywhere. As I'm only 4 foot 11 inches tall (or small, whichever way you look at it), this wasn't the easiest position for me to be in. Without the cooperation of Abbie directing her feet through the holes in the trolley seat, it was an impossible task for me to get her in there. I very nearly got one foot in the seat but she was doing everything in her power to stop the other one going anywhere near. It was then a battle of wills to see who was going to give up first. After several unsuccessful attempts, and rather than using my elbow to 'encourage' her to bend in the middle and as the blood slowly drained from my arms, I could do no more than put her down. This left me no choices as I had to get the shopping done – the cupboard was bare and we were completely out of wine! I decided at this point to play my joker card: sweets!

Now, I know it's wrong to reward bad behaviour, but it's surprising how a packet of sweets can remind children how easy it is to bend in the middle again. So, with her sweets in her hand, we tried once more. Not a problem this time: she was now the perfect shape again to fit into the trolley seat. Abbie was now more than happy concentrating on trying to open her packet of sweets, as, to give myself a little more time, I'd left her with the packet unopened. Sounds a bit cruel, I know, but those five minutes can make all the difference when you get to the tills.

She was working very hard to get the packet open, and this got me part way down the first aisle. After that, she was starting to get a little bit frustrated, so I opened the packet up for her, making the smallest hole I could, hoping that they'd last her a bit longer. For now, she seemed happy with that. Now, the one packet of sweets wasn't going to give me that much time, so I had to be quick, knowing full well that once all the sweets were gone I could be in trouble. I managed to get down another three aisles before she'd finally eaten them all. At this point, though, she was still in good spirits. We'd just about finished the shopping and would have soon been outside had there not been so many people queuing at the tills. I was desperately trying to keep her entertained by singing songs and playing 'peek-a-boo', but I knew it was only a matter of time now before she'd be wanting to get out of that trolley. She was beginning to get more and more agitated by the second. We now had the added bonus of the E-numbers in the sweets that she'd just eaten, so I knew this wasn't going to be pretty! I was right. Her eyes suddenly looked a little glazed and her cheeks changed to a pinky-purply colour. It looked like my time was up because Abbie had now started trying to climb out of the trolley and was well on her way until I grabbed hold of her feet to 'encourage' her to stay where she was. She glared at me. It was a look I'd seen before, and unfortunately at this point I knew we were in for a full-scale paddy. The noise she made next was probably loud enough for the whole supermarket to hear, and she was now more purple than pink.

Understandably, at this point, people were beginning to stare, some finding it quite entertaining I'm sure, but there were also a few sympathetic looks from people who had obviously been there themselves, and a good few looks of disgust from those who hadn't. I did try to talk to Abbie but it was no use – she couldn't hear me over all the noise she was making. As she got louder, redder and snottier, the situation was pretty much out of my control. I decided it was probably best to just ignore her and concentrate on getting out as quick as I could. I dread to think how many people were staring at us by now, but I could feel lots of eyes on me. I was so hoping that there wasn't anyone about who might have recognised us.

At last it was my turn at the till. I was trying my best to get the shopping out of the trolley, going as fast as I could, but not quite fast enough, as the noise level at this point was quite painful to the ear. I could feel myself getting hotter and hotter as I was throwing my shopping on to the counter. The assistant was trying her best to make conversation with me, but I couldn't hear a thing she was saying over Abbie's yelling. Finally, I had all my shopping in bags, and all I had to do now was pay and then I could get out of there. I was shaking slightly and fumbling around with my purse, dropping it several times, eventually managing to pay the lady. Thank goodness we were finally on our way out. Pushing the trolley as quickly as I could, with my head down to hide my incredibly red face, I made my way towards the exit. But as I approached the doors, I noticed something: it had suddenly gone very quiet, and my ears were no longer ringing. It was as if she'd been switched off – the little monkey had finally shut up. And was that a smile I could see on her face? Indeed it was.

After unloading the shopping into the boot, all I had to do now was get her out of the trolley and back into the car. Ah, the car seat! How difficult could that be? At least she was happy again and very pleased that I'd finally taken her out of the shopping trolley. Until she spotted the car seat! Within seconds, she'd managed to turned herself back into an ironing board – only this time I was having none of it. I'm out of sweets by now and I can see from the corner of my eye that my shopping trolley is just setting off, rolling down the gradual slope of the supermarket car park. I really had no choice this time but to 'encourage' her into the seat as fast as I possibly could. As I clicked the fastener on the car seat, I quickly turned round to see my trolley, which by now was gathering speed and heading towards a beautiful looking BMW. I set off running across the car park as fast as I could. It was at that point I knew, without a doubt, that somebody somewhere was looking over me, because there was no way I was ever going to catch that trolley before it reached the BMW. Then an amazingly lucky thing happened: the trolley went over a big crack in the tarmac and stopped dead in its tracks. I couldn't believe it.

'Yes, thank you, thank you!' I shouted up towards the sky.

I ran towards it, drawing a little more attention to myself and getting a few strange looks from confused people. I didn't care anymore. My street credit had long gone. I quickly took my trolley back to retrieve my pound coin. On returning to the car, I couldn't quite believe it, but Abbie had fallen asleep. Aww bless. She'd obviously worn her little self out. Right then, home for a coffee, or should I risk putting her into the pram and going to the café?! Don't be ridiculous. So home it was, for coffee and maybe something a little stronger.

Words of Wisdom

As for shopping with toddlers, it's not really what they want to do, is it? And can you blame them? Have you felt how hard and uncomfortable those trolley seats are? I suppose the one saving grace is that the majority of little ones riding in them will still be in nappies, giving them a little bit of padding and hopefully making it a slightly softer ride.

When you think about it, they've worked so very hard to get those little legs working – months and months of practice, some of them even years. So it's not surprising, then, that, after all the effort they've put in, the last thing they want to be doing is to be stopped in their tracks.

Thank goodness for online shopping – what a great invention that one was. Such a shame it wasn't widely available back then. If, for some reason, you can't do your shopping online and babysitters are not an option, I suggest you read this chapter through again before you make your final decision on leaving for the supermarket with a toddler in tow. Maybe then you might agree with me. Letting them explore your home isn't such a bad idea after all.

From my experiences, sweets and E-numbers really do make a difference. I've seen perfectly well behaved children turn into monsters almost instantly after drinking or eating any. Think very carefully of the consequences before you give them out; it may be a quick fix to a problem, but often the long-term after-effects are far worse.

•

16

Here comes another

After a six-and-a-half-year gap, I'd finally plucked up the courage to do it all again. Abbie's birth and the three years of sleep deprivation were, by now, a distant memory.

I'd been told at the hospital, after the way Abbie's birth had gone, should I have any more children, a caesarean section would be offered to me. Perhaps they weren't up for another fifty-six hours of labour – I know I certainly wasn't! This in mind, I was feeling rather brave on my first visit to see the midwife. Alas, the brave feeling was to be short-lived because, seemingly, as a good few years had now passed since my last labour, they felt it would be best to just see how I went on with a natural delivery. I was panic-stricken; suddenly all the nightmare moments of Abbie's birth came flooding back. This really wasn't what I wanted to hear at this point, only twelve weeks into my pregnancy; I had a lot of time to worry about it, and feeling sick from morning till night wasn't helping me with my positive attitude. I did keep on trying to convince myself all would be fine this time. You never know, this delivery might just be idyllic, just like the ones you hear about, where the baby pops out in no time at all and the mother hadn't even realised she was in labour.

As much as I loved being pregnant, the sickness in my second pregnancy was far worse than it had been with Abbie. It never let up from waking up in a morning until going to bed at night. It was a joy to go to sleep as it gave me a break from feeling so awful. So the moment I got Abbie into her bed at 7.30, I then went straight to mine. The great news this time, though: I wasn't doing it alone as by now a good few of my family and friends had finally decided it was time for them to start their own families. Stacey was now also expecting her first baby and was due three weeks before me – very exciting for us both.

We were both due in the January of 2000, but Stacey's little boy, Tom, arrived two weeks early on 28th December 1999. After a relatively pleasant pregnancy, she then went through a traumatic delivery, similar to what I had with Abbie. Then, at last after nine months and two weeks of being a strange shade of green and feeling completely dreadful, I was taken into hospital on the evening of 28th January to be induced. The baby was now two weeks overdue, and with each day I'd gone over my due date I was becoming more and more anxious. How big was this baby going to be? Abbie was only six pounds three ounces, and I'd had enough trouble trying to get her out! It felt like I'd been pregnant forever.

After being induced that evening the labour pains came on thick and fast. I was finding it quite difficult to contain myself as I was in a ward with three other ladies, with only a curtain around each bed to separate us from one another. The other ladies were mainly there for bed rest due to complications in their pregnancies, so the last thing I wanted to do was make a fuss and disturb them. However, as the pains got steadily worse it was becoming increasingly difficult. The only thing I could do was to grip on to the bedhead and bite my arm!

So when the midwife came and looked around the curtain she did seem a little shocked. 'Joanne are you okay? I think we'd better get you examined and get your husband to come back in.'

Gary had been sent home earlier as we weren't yet on the labour ward. She scurried off, returning with a measly paracetamol, compensated for by the news that Gary was on his way.

Now, there were a couple of complications going on this particular night. The first one was that the labour ward was full. This meant that they were unable to give me a labour room, which also meant that, other than that measly paracetamol, no further pain relief could be administered. Not good news for me as the paracetamol appeared to have done nothing. I was in just as much, if not more pain now and I was beginning to run out of arm space to bite!

The other problem was the weather. It was horrendous that night: the gale-force winds and driving rain had resulted in one of the windows being blown in on one of the other wards. Understandably, all the staff seemed very preoccupied with this. Now, I'm not one to make a fuss and I was still trying my best to be as quiet as I could. This, perhaps, resulted in me being ever so slightly forgotten about, at least for a little while anyway.

It was reassuring that Gary was on his way back. On arriving at the hospital, he wasn't best pleased to find me alone behind my curtain, desperately trying to keep quiet with each contraction. We'd been here before, only now we were older and wiser. So off he went to find somebody to 'have a word' with. I'm not overly sure what he said, but he soon returned pushing a wheelchair.

'Come on, love, let's get you on to that labour ward. They're waiting for us.'

I was in too much pain to ask what he'd said, and before I knew what was going on we were on our way to the delivery suite whether they were ready for us or not. I'd never seen Gary so assertive – I guess he didn't want a repeat performance of last time either. As he wheeled me down to the ward we were met by another midwife who seemed to be expecting us – she had managed to find us a free room.

As soon as we were in there I spotted the gas and air on the wall. I was out of the wheelchair in seconds. I grabbed it, putting it straight into my mouth, breathing it in for as long as I could. At last, after the four hours I'd just gone through, this was like a dream come true. I thought I was never going to make it to the delivery suite. The midwife was reading through my notes and looking the other way and therefore hadn't noticed what I was doing.

'Okay, Joanne, I know you had a hard time with your last baby, but this isn't going to be anything like that,' she said in a reassuring voice as she turned to look at me.

When she saw I was on the bed already with the gas and air in my mouth, she started to smile. 'Great, Joanne, you just get stuck in with that, and after that next contraction, I can put the mask on it for you.' She looked at Gary and they both started laughing.

I had just put the whole tube in my mouth – I didn't even realise there was a mask for it. They all had a good chuckle at that, and before I had my next contraction she quickly fitted the mask.

'Is that easier for you now, Joanne?' she asked as I sucked in as much as I could. It definitely was much easier. These contractions were big ones though. I must be at least nine or even ten centimetres dilated by now, I thought to myself.

'You're four centimetres, Joanne, so we're going to put a little monitor on the baby's head to register its heartbeat, just so we can see how it's coping with the labour.'

Four centimetres, is that all? My god, I thought I'd have been at least eight or nine. Does that mean these contractions are going to get even worse then? Maybe they might like to put a monitor on *my* head, see how I'm coping with labour! I'd forgotten it was this bad. Had I really gone and done it again? What on earth was I thinking? I must be mad. I could feel the panic rushing through me but the arrival of another contraction temporarily took my mind off things.

The heart monitor was attached to the baby's head, and we could now hear its little heart beating away. I was pretty preoccupied with the pain but I did notice that a few more people seemed to be appearing in our room – first another midwife then a couple of doctors came in. They kept looking and chatting amongst themselves. I couldn't help feeling that they were all starting to look a bit concerned. Gary looked at me and squeezed my hand.

'It's alright, love, don't worry.'

But it all felt a bit too familiar to me. The arrival of a third doctor confirmed that we were right to be concerned: they weren't happy with the baby's heartbeat. This was an indication that the baby was in distress, so they needed to move quickly. It was decided immediately: they were going to have to perform an emergency caesarean and in no time at all we were off back down to theatre. I was given an epidural because there wasn't time for anaesthetic. Gary was back in his blues and the room was once again filled with people, rushing around, plugging in machines and monitors and generally dashing from one thing to another. It seemed that time was definitely of the essence.

Well, at least they'll be no pushing this time then – I suppose that's got to be a bonus, I tried to tell myself to keep my mind off what was about to happen. I was looking very closely at the doctors' eyes above their blue masks to see if they seemed to be panicking. Difficult to tell, really, but *I* was panicking. They were going to cut my stomach open, and I was still awake! Once again I could feel my heart beating fast in my head. I tried to avoid looking up at the huge light on the ceiling as I was sure I could see the reflection of what they were doing in it! They did actually have some music playing, which was quite nice and all seemed relatively calm compared to when Abbie had been born.

There was quite a bit of pushing and pulling, and at one point it did feel like someone was doing their washing up in my stomach –

something I'd heard other people say a caesarean felt like – but apart from that, really quite painless.

Then, in what seemed like no time at all, the midwife said, 'Congratulations, you two. It's a boy.'

And there he was.

At 6am on Saturday 29th January 2000, James Harry was finally born. I couldn't believe it – a boy. A boy! I would have been more than happy with another girl, but a boy? How lucky were we! They passed James over to Gary.

'Well it looks like nappies are going to be a whole new ball game, then,' he said with a huge smile on his face and a little tear in his eye.

He weighed seven pounds and two ounces, not massive but plenty big enough. Nearly a whole pound bigger than Abbie. They were a good while stitching and stapling me up and when they did finally take the screen down I tried to avoid looking in the direction of my tummy. I can remember very clearly shaking uncontrollably whilst they were trying to sort out my tummy and thinking, I wish I could keep still, otherwise they're going to be making a bit of a mess with these stitches. I did have plenty of stitches and a very sore tummy, but hey, at least I could sit down this time. As we were in the recovery room for quite some time the midwife came into see us all.

'Now then, Joanne, are we breastfeeding baby?'

Oh no, here we go again, bloody breastfeeding, 'breast is best'. Is it really though!? Even when you're clearly rubbish at it? Well, I suppose I had to give it go as I'd done it for Abbie, and if I didn't now do it for James it wouldn't be fair, now would it? I couldn't cope with that guilt. I'd have to give it a try. Anyway, Stacey now had Tom: she'd been breastfeeding him for five weeks and was finding it easy – although she did seem have enough milk to feed everyone's babies.

'Yes, I'll give it a go,' I finally answered.

Having now been all stitched and stapled back together, we were taken back up on to the ward. I'm not sure what they'd given me but I was so excited. Maybe it was sheer relief that I'd survived another birth, and with two children now I wouldn't have to go through it ever again. I couldn't quite believe I'd had a boy; I really did expect it to be another girl. The ward was buzzing with activity as it had been an extremely busy night on the delivery suite: there had been six babies born, all by caesarean with only one other lady having a natural birth – and she'd had twins! So there was plenty going on and it was very noisy, but that didn't bother me. I was more than happy, all drugged up and smiling away to myself behind my curtain, every so often having a little peek at little James asleep at the side of me in his cot. I couldn't wait for Abbie to seem him. Gary had gone home to get showered and make some phone calls to let everyone know the news. Grandma was looking after Abbie so he was going to bring them both back so that she could be the first to see her little brother. Eventually we were moved into our own room, which was great. I made sure at this point that my bed was on the lowest setting. I didn't want a repeat performance of last time, as pole-vaulting perhaps wouldn't be a good move with a newly-stapled-up tummy.

A little later on that day, as I was just starting to nod off, the door flew open and in skipped Abbie with a huge smile on her face. She ran over to me and then very shyly looked over at the cot that James was in.

'Go on, have a look at your little brother, then.'

Standing on her tiptoes, she could just about see over the top of the cot. She stood staring at him for a little while, looking all shy for a minute or two, then turned to me and asked, 'Did they really cut your tummy open with a knife, Mummy?'

Probably wasn't what I was expecting her to say, but I suppose she was right, though I hadn't really thought about it, until then actually. 'Well, yes, I think they have, but now they've got James out they have stitched it all back up again.'

'Can I have a look?' she replied excitedly.

I wasn't sure that I was ready to look yet. So I suggested she had a cuddle with James and hoped that would keep her busy for a while – long enough for her to forget all about looking at my stitches anyway. She seemed to be enjoy that ... until he started to cry and fidget about. Then she quickly passed him over to Grandma, who had been patiently waiting for her turn.

After everyone had gone home I ventured to the toilet – a much more pleasant experience than it had been after having Abbie. I think I was still quite high on all the drugs they'd given me as I kept giggling to myself. I quickly glanced in the mirror: I looked different, but I wasn't really sure why. Then it hit me – how had I not noticed before? I was no longer that shade of green I'd been for the last nine months. It was the first time in about two-hundred-and-eighty-four days that I didn't feel sick! I started giggling again. Forgetting where I was, and why, for a second, I then threw my hands in the air to celebrate. Obviously, this was far too much movement for my newly stitched tummy, so I very quickly put them down again and started singing instead.

'Cel-e-brate good times, come on! Yar-hoo!'

'Are you alright in there, Joanne?' a voice asked from outside my door. It looked like the poor midwife had been waiting outside the bathroom for me all this time, whilst I'd been singing and giggling away. No wonder she was starting to get a little concerned. I came out of the toilet with a slightly red face.

'Yes, I'm fine. I don't feel sick anymore. It's great.'

James and I had another three days' stay in hospital, after which time they decided it would be okay for us both to go home. I think it would be safe to say that birthing plan number two hadn't really come off, then either!

17

Is breast really best?

It would appear that all of a sudden and as if by magic, after waiting for over seven years, all our friends and family were at last beginning to produce babies of their own. Both Gary's brother and mine now had children of their own, Stacey had Tom, who was just five weeks older than James, and Maria, another one of our friends, had Sam – there was only three weeks between him and James. Even my two school friends had finally taken the plunge: Ellen had her little girl, Annabelle, who was eighteen months old, and Alice was expecting in May that year. I finally had some company along the way.

This little story begins on a cold February morning. Having already done the school run with Abbey, Stacey and I were being very brave that day as we'd decided to go together into town to do some shopping with the boys. We were both very loaded down with prams, car seats, bags full of nappies and all things you needed to have when going anywhere with a newborn. The one good thing, though, was that we were both breastfeeding, so we didn't need to be making up and taking bottles of milk. After quite some time going back and forth into the house, trying to make sure we hadn't forgotten anything and amazingly fitting two prams in the boot of a Matiz (very small car), we were finally on our way and very pleased with ourselves that we'd actually managed to leave the house, as it was still only 10.30.

Stacey, as I mentioned earlier, had taken to breastfeeding like a duck to water. Tom only seemed to take about ten minutes with each feed, then they were all done for about three to four hours.

'Eh, you've actually finished already?' I'd say. I was amazed by this, as I was usually still trying to get James latched on at this point. Then would follow a long and drawn-out ordeal where James would feed for about thirty minutes then fall asleep. I'd then spend a good few minutes trying to wake him up in order to get him to have some more. He'd eventually wake up, but only for about ten minutes, then the same thing would happen again. This process would usually go on for about one to one-and-a-half hours, by which time he was neither completely full nor ready to go back to sleep again. So I was never really quite sure if it was safe to leave the house with him.

On arriving in the city centre, we were lucky enough to find a parking space just near to the entrance and the lifts to all the shops. Unloading of prams, car seats, baby bags and babies then began. Eventually we arrived in Boots, and Stacey kept sticking her head into Tom's pram.

'Oh dear, I think Tom's filled his nappy. We'd best just nip into the mother and baby changing room before we start, so he doesn't stink the whole shop out!'

As he was a fully breastfed baby, you definitely knew when a change was due. This was, without doubt, a good idea, both for him and anyone else around. James, thankfully at this point, was still fast asleep. When Stacey went to change Tom's nappy she realised that he'd almost totally boycotted his nappy and had completely covered his vest instead. We both started hunting around in our huge baby bags only to find that between us we didn't have a spare vest. We had spare everything else – and enough nappies for ten babies – but not a vest. As we were in Boots, I had a brainwave. 'No problem, I'll buy you one from here.'

'What a good idea,' she agreed.

So off I went, leaving Stacey with James and Tom in the mother and baby room and eventually returning with a vest.

'Thanks, that's great, but James is just starting to stir a little, I think.'

'I'll try to feed him, then, whilst we're in here. There's no point getting out there and then having to come back in.'

I took him out of his pram and started to feed him. Having sat there for about thirty minutes, James had done his usual and fed for a bit and then fallen asleep.

'Come on, then, let's get going. That'll have to do, we can't sit here all day whilst he feeds for as long as he usually does.'

But James just wouldn't stop crying. Once more I tried to feed him, but he wasn't having it at all. He was thrashing around and getting redder and redder.

'I think he's still hungry, you know,' Stacey said.

'Yes, I think you're right, but I'm clearly out of milk. What am I going to do?'

At this point Stacey looked over at me, obviously thinking the same thing as I was.

'No!' we both blurted out at the same time.

'I know, don't they sell milk in a carton now, all just ready to go? I'm sure I've seen an advert on the telly,' Stacey said.

'Yes, yes I think they do. Maybe I could try him with some.'

Again, the fact we were in Boots was very helpful. So off she nipped this time, leaving me with a very noisy James. Tom was still fast asleep, regardless of all the screaming that James was now doing. Stacey soon returned, smiling.

'I've got some, and here's a ready-sterilised bottle too.'

James couldn't get it in fast enough: he drank the whole bottle, hardly stopping to breathe and afterwards letting out the longest burp I've ever heard. At last, he was full and happy. As quickly as I could I changed his nappy, then started to get him back in his pram so that we could at last start our shopping. I was just tucking him in when we heard a little noise coming from Tom's pram. We both looked at each other.

'Oh no, I don't believe it!'

Now Tom was hungry, so we sat down once more whilst Stacey fed him, after which we heard that all too familiar sound of him filling his nappy for a second time. So it was then back on the changing mat with him. Stacey and I just kept looking at each other and shaking our heads in disbelief. We'd now been in the mother and baby room for nearly two hours! Our money had just about run out on the parking. In fact, by the time we'd got them both back into their prams and waited for the lift back up to the car park we were actually ten minutes late.

So that's what we did in town that day. We spent the whole two hours in the mother and baby room. As if that wasn't bad enough, when we got back to the car, we'd managed to pick ourselves up a parking ticket! How very unkind that seemed. Shopping is still not one of mine or Stacey's favourite things to do, and perhaps that's down to that morning in February. We did, however, appeal our parking ticket and it turned out in the end we didn't have to pay it. I think they put it down as 'an unfortunate sequence of events'.

Let's face it, I don't think you could make up a story like that.

Words of Wisdom

I think the main thing to come out of this for me was that I no longer needed to beat myself up about breastfeeding. I was clearly rubbish at it and perhaps it was best left to the naturals, the ones with more than enough milk, possibly enough to feed everyone's babies.

When venturing out with newborns it's always a good idea to take along plenty of spare clothes because, tiny as they are, sick and poo can strike at any time, often when you're least expecting it.

Oh, and there is such a thing as a car park attendant with a heart.

18
Cruel to be kind

James seemed to grasp the idea of sleep slightly better than Abbie had, and it wasn't until he was about eighteen months old that things started to change. He seemed to be getting into a habit of waking up in the night more and more; it was like having a newborn all over again. This could have had something to do with the fact that he'd quite suddenly stopped eating solid food. He had always, up until then, enjoyed his meals, most of which I'd carefully prepared for him and frozen into ice-cube trays. For some unknown reason, James had decided he didn't want to eat them anymore and that he'd go back to having only milk. Milk for breakfast, dinner, tea and supper!

The refusal of solid food was a very messy business and after several weeks of battles, paddies and tears, from us both, he left me with no choice but to give in. Having tried in vain to prise open his lips with the spoon and failing miserably to convince him that the spoon was actually a train, plane or a bus, I then moved on to singing several renditions of all his favourite songs whilst dancing around the kitchen. This performance continued for weeks but despite all my efforts nothing seemed to be working. Every now and then he'd open his mouth only to lull me into thinking he was actually going to eat something. He'd then take great pleasure in blowing raspberries and spitting it all back out again, usually in my direction, as this seemed to amuse him – a lot. Then would follow the long sessions of cleaning up all this wasted food which was usually everywhere. The high chair caught most of the meal because it would slide down the bars and get caught in the hinges, something that if not removed straight away (especially if it contained mashed potatoes) would dry like concrete and was almost impossible to get clean. It could be on the floor, worktops, and I always managed to have a considerable amount on me.

Then I would start on James, often finding food in his ears from when he turned away to dodge the spoon at the very last second. There was always plenty up his nose and in his hair. Regardless of the extra-large bib I had for him, he still needed to be stripped and changed from head to foot – sometimes it was just easier to put him straight into the bath. The final straw came one afternoon when after an hour or so unsuccessfully trying to get some food down him, I turned away for only a second or two looking for a cloth.

On turning back around I was mortified to find the dish was now upside down on the floor whilst James was patting his hands on the high chair table in the remains of his dinner – it was splatting and spraying everywhere, and he was singing and smiling all the while. This day I remember well as it was the breaking point for me.

So we were back to the staple diet of milk. The only problem then was that he was waking up at least three to six times in the night as he was no doubt a little bit peckish. A bottle of milk seemed to suffice for about three hours, then we were up again for some more ... This went on for a good while. James would have himself a nice little power nap in the afternoons, which refreshed him so that he had plenty of energy and was ready to do it all again that next night – whilst I was slowly turning into a zombie. My eyelids were once more getting a lot of attention as they were now the focal point of my whole face.

One day, a close friend, Sally, told me she'd read somewhere that if you stop offering milk in the night and just offer them boring water instead, eventually they'll break the habit and stop waking up. She continued to explain that I would need to be strong and ignore him, maybe even leaving him to cry for a little while, before eventually going in to him with the water only, no milk. Of course, I came up with all the excuses as to why I, The Perfect Mum, couldn't possibly do that.

'I can't leave him crying in the night. He might wake Abbie up, and she has to be up for school every morning.'

'She'll be fine. Anyway, apparently, it doesn't even take that long, just a few nights,' Sally told me.

'But ... but ... I just can't. What if he starves to death? He's not eaten any solid foods through the day for weeks now' was my weak reply.

So on I battled with this game for a few more weeks. Then, one morning after being woken nine – yes, nine – times, I finally reached my wits' end. I'd had enough of walking round in a daze, being bad tempered and bursting into tears all the time. So that morning I rang Sally.

'Okay, Sally, what do I have to do?'

'Well, when he wakes up leave him for two minutes to cry. Then go in to him with the water, and each time just add another two minutes on before you go back in.'

'Oh, okay then. That doesn't sound too bad.'

I had to be firm with myself because listening to him cry and shout 'Mummy!' did break my heart. But I was exhausted and I was sick of people telling me how tired I looked. So I stuck to my guns. When he woke up that night I went in to him with only water.

Night one: I gave him the water, he sucked away on it for a second or two, then dragged it out of his mouth in disgust, realising it wasn't milk, and instantly started crying again. He cried for about forty-five minutes that first time then eventually fell back asleep. On waking a second time that evening I did the same, another forty-five minutes; then it started to get a little less each time. The second night was much the same, but not for quite as long. In his rage, a bottle or two got thrown out of the cot in protest, and on one occasion I had to swerve pretty quick to get out of its way. Often by the time I got back into bed Gary had usually pinched my pillow to put over his ears. But I was determined to crack this. I felt I'd done my fair share of sleepless nights – and I'd started it now, so I had to stay with it, which is exactly what I did, very nearly giving in a couple of times at 2am but then talking myself back round. I was going to give it at least five nights. Then if it didn't work? Well, if this didn't work, I didn't really know what I was going to do. Move out? Get a nanny?

Fortunately for me it was a success and it turned out to be all worthwhile, as after only four nights of this, I'd cracked it. I was amazed because by the end of the week he was not only sleeping through again but he was also back eating solid food.

Why hadn't I just done this six months ago? I could have saved myself a lot of pain. Listening to plenty of paddies and a good amount of crying – even the bruise from the flying bottle I didn't quite get out of the way of in time – was all very much worth it, because I'd done it, stood my ground and it had worked. Believe it or not, whilst all that was going on, Abbie never woke up, not once. And, perhaps even more surprisingly, James didn't die of starvation.

Words of Wisdom

Never underestimate a trained toddler – they're cleverer than you think. They may look sweet and innocent, and as beautiful as those eyes may be, they know exactly what they're doing. When it's a battle of wills you're entering into, avoid eye contact at all times, otherwise they have won.

19

Never compare

Now, it would seem, was a great time to have a baby, as all of a sudden we were meeting up with our friends through the day with their children to go to the park and play gyms and to look around farms. No longer were we having to decline on an evening invitation to go out because now, surprisingly, no one else was going out either. We weren't the only ones staying home on a Saturday night anymore, and it felt good.

Stacey, Maria and I spent a great deal of time together in those early days after the boys were born. Having had our babies within three weeks of each other, we were all going through the same things and it was great to have the company this time round. I didn't feel as lonely as I'd done with Abbie as a newborn. We could talk about how we were feeling and discuss what we were going through – perhaps more importantly, laugh about things together. Catching up and chatting with a coffee whilst the boys played together was good fun all round for everybody, exchanging notes and advice with each other – and you can't help but compare.

Tom and Sam, Stacey and Maria's boys, were both sitting up by the time they were six or seven months old. James – unlike Abbie, who walked before she was one – had absolutely no interest in or intention of sitting up when he was six months old. He seemed more than happy to be lying down on the floor or carried around every-where by me, and who could blame him? Why walk when you can be carried? When Tom and Sam were sat up playing on the floor with their toys I'd often put James down at the side of them, just to see if he'd get the idea. He didn't; he only flopped straight down on to his back, perfectly happy with himself. I mean, it wasn't as if he was frustrated and crying; he was more than happy lying down kicking his legs around. To make things worse, though, he then started doing a caterpillar-like movement with his legs. I suppose it was a bit like body-popping but lying down. He would lift both feet up into the air, which in turn made his bum pop up and back down again (hence the caterpillar comparison). In time, he became pretty good at this and soon was able to move himself around the floor, often picking up quite some speed. It was indeed very strange to watch; I'd never seen any other babies doing this before. This did show if anybody came around to visit, as when they caught sight of James 'caterpillaring' about, they were always very intrigued as to what he was actually doing.

'What's all that about, then?' asked Phil, Stacey's husband, a bit shocked when he first saw James doing it. 'I've never seen that before. Did Tom do that? I can't remember seeing him.'

It was most unique, so by the time the other two boys were starting to pull themselves up on to the furniture and taking their first steps, James was still 'caterpillaring' around on the floor. He seemed to have no interest whatsoever in being upright. To be honest, for long enough I wasn't too concerned at all, but as time went by and the boys were all coming up to being a year old, James was still showing no signs of even sitting sit up. At this point I was beginning to get just a little bit worried. I think Stacey and Maria were too, as when I expressed my concern to them, they both agreed that it might be a good idea to take him to the doctors.

'Take him, just to get him checked out,' they both said simultaneously.

It didn't help matters that Abbie had been up and walking since way before she was one – although I did realise that she was a relatively early walker, and that all her bouncing in the swing had probably contributed to that. Then it hit me: the swing! How could I have forgotten about the swing? Yes, that would be perfect to encourage him on to his feet. I just needed to remember where I'd put it, eventually locating it in the depths of the loft after several hours of searching.

Whilst in there, we came across plenty of baby photos of Abbie, making us realise that we hadn't taken half as many pictures of James – there just didn't seem to be the time anymore. We must remember to take more pictures of him from now on, Gary and I both agreed as we finally emerged from the loft, very excited about getting James into the bouncy swing, as we felt sure that this was just what he needed. He wasn't too sure about it at first, but we persevered, patiently waiting for him to start to bounce around like Abbie did.

Each time we put him in, he would just hang there, looking like a puppet that needed some string.

'Come on, James. It's great fun!' I would say excitedly whilst I demonstrated bouncing up and down in front of him!

But no, he just looked at me with a worried expression on his face. He wouldn't even put his feet down on the floor. We tried pushing him, spinning him around, but he just hated everything about it. More often than not he'd start to cry, so we always ended up having to lift him out and lay him back down on the floor where he was happy. We couldn't understand it at all. What was wrong with him?

I'd have days and nights when I worried a lot about him, but as he seemed very happy in himself I kept putting off taking him to the doctors. I really didn't want to take him as I was frightened of what they might tell me. So we just kept plodding on, and James continued entertaining many people with his horizontal body-popping.

Then, one day a few weeks down the line, right out of the blue, James decided he was going to sit up. I came into the lounge with his breakfast that morning and there he was: sat bolt upright on the carpet, as if he'd been doing it for months.

'James, you can do it! Thank goodness!' I shouted as I ran over to him.

I was that excited I think I made him jump. He just looked at me as if to say, yes of course I can, what's your problem, you silly woman? Then not too long after that at around fifteen months old, a day that we'll never forget, he finally ventured into the world of walking.

Words of Wisdom

Comparing: as tempting as it is, try not to do it. You'll save yourself a whole lot of heartache, because you just can't rush these things. They'll do it when they're ready, not when you think it's time, and they're all so very different. Even your own two children can be complete opposites.

Perhaps most importantly, what's the rush? A horizontal toddler is much easier to keep up with, as once they find their feet, your job looking after them suddenly becomes a great deal harder. Indeed, all that time I spent worrying, and just because the other two were already up and about. He was absolutely fine, just taking his time – something that I was going to have to get used to, with James!!!

20

Birthdays, cakes and party bags

Birthdays are a large chapter. The main areas I want to cover are:

1. Parties
2. Party bags
3. Birthday cakes

Parties

Your children's first birthday party is quite an important one – well, it is to you, but your one-year-old isn't really going to know much about it (Abbie and James both slept through theirs). The first three parties are mostly for close family and friends, but once they start nursery or school it's a whole new ball game.

After the first few birthday parties, when I'd invited all their little friends around to our house, I soon started to realise that it's not that much fun having fifteen or so little ones trashing your house – least not for you, anyway. It's a far better idea to take them all somewhere else, away from home, maybe somewhere that's geared up for this sort of thing. Thank goodness for the Wacky Warehouse; this was to be the venue for James's fifth birthday party.

Now, having only moved into the area about six months earlier, we were still getting to know people. James had only been at school for four months so when I asked him which friends he'd like to invite to his party, I wasn't entirely sure who they all were, or, indeed, which mum they all belonged to. Nevertheless, he took invitations for twelve, of which eight replied positively. As the party day drew nearer, and having still not heard from the remaining four children, I decided to let James invite another four friends to make up the numbers. He did this, and luckily all four of them could come. This was great, but then the day before the party the parents of the original four we'd first invited all decided to let me know that their kids would be coming after all. This would now mean that, added to the six family friends that were already coming, we now had a grand total of twenty-two children able to come! This may not have been too bad; at least they weren't coming to my house. But when we got to the 'Wacky' that day, it did seem extremely busy.

A young girl came over to talk to us as we arrived. 'Hi there. We have another two parties on today, so it's a bit busy!' she shouted over the noise.

Busy was an understatement. It was heaving, and the noise level was unbelievable. With all the screaming and shouting going on it was all most impossible to hear yourself think.

As the mums and dads began to arrive, I could feel my heart sinking as their kids threw their shoes at me and ran off into the play area. I'd thought that with them being so young maybe one or two of the parents might just stay and watch/help. But no, not a chance: they couldn't get out of there fast enough, more or less pushing their kids in, and then they were off.

'See you in two hours, thanks.'

And so began two hours of hell! The fact that I didn't even know most of these children didn't help at all. As one mum left I heard her saying to her son, 'Now, remember, these children are your friends. Please don't hurt any of them, I don't want any fighting.'

What did she mean? I wanted to ask her but it was too late as she, too, was gone. Now, things might not have been that bad if they'd all come in their school uniforms as at least then I may of had a slightly better chance of been able to identify them amongst the other children's parties in there. Naturally, they'd all come dressed in their party clothes, making it impossible to differentiate them from the other two parties that were now in full swing. I felt quite dizzy trying to track them all down. Apart from James and the few family friends, I had very little clue as to who was actually with our lot. I'd put my mum on guard at the door to make sure there were no escapees – although my mother had even less idea than I who was actually with our party, so this wasn't very easy for her as she had to keep calling across to me, over the screaming and shouting, 'Is this one of ours?'

In the end I left her to it as an argument had started in the ball pool: there was a little bit of rivalry between our party and one of the others. One of our boys was calling them names, and it wasn't going down well at all. I stood shouting from the side for quite some time, but it was useless: they couldn't hear me above the noise. In the end I just had to get in, as by now a small fight had broken out. I threw myself through the hole in the nets – perhaps one of those times when being so small can be an advantage.

Climbing up to the top of the ladder, I then slid down the slide and, on landing in the middle of the ball pool, I grabbed the two boys.

'What are you doing, boys? This is a party.'

I then heard a faint voice in the back ground.

'Excuse me, excuse me.' Looking behind me I saw one of the assistants. 'You're not allowed in the play area,' she proceeded to tell me.

'I know, but they were fighting and I had to do something about it,' I explained as I waded my way through the balls.

With my red face and the two boys in tow, I made my way to the exit. The noise seemed to have dropped considerably and, looking around, I saw that everyone appeared to be looking at me.

'Now, who are you with?' I asked the boy.

He pointed over to the biggest man I'd ever seen. He was sat in the corner, oblivious, reading his paper with a coffee. Taking in a deep breath, I went over with the boy. I wasn't too sure what I was going to say to him, but thought it best to just open my mouth and see what came out.

'Excuse me, sorry to bother you, but your son's been fighting in the ball pool. I think he needs some time out.' This was my best effort.

He looked at me like I'd fallen out of the sky. I turned to walk away and, literally a few seconds later, the boy ran past me and went straight back in to the ball pool. That worked well then, I thought, as I looked back at his dad who was still engrossed in his paper. Having had a word with 'our boy', who I'd never met before, I then thought it was easier to just let him go back in. I felt I had quite enough to do keeping my eyes on the rest of our group. It was kicking off all over the place, just far too many kids for the one play area. I kept going from one part to another, sorting one little incident out then quickly moving on to the next. It was carnage.

Meanwhile, my mum was still standing her ground, guarding the door. She did make a few mistakes here and there, refusing to let a couple of children go out of the door until their parents appeared. Turned out they weren't actually with our party and just wanted to get to their mum and dad, who were sat having a drink in the pub. I'm afraid this didn't go down at all well with the parents, but as my mum had always been able to handle herself, I left her to it.

Then, thank goodness, they blew the whistle, which meant it was the end of playing and time for tea. They all came dashing out of the play area and into the room upstairs where the tables were all set for teatime. It was a great relief to get them all together in one place – well, it was once we'd actually found them all, as a couple of the boys thought it might be funny to play a trick on me and hide themselves in the ball pool. Like I needed that! Mum and I sat down, both a little stunned, I think. We didn't speak; we just sat staring into space. After about thirty minutes, and whilst they were all still sat eating their tea, I quickly glanced at my watch: only three quarters of an hour to go, yes, we were nearly there. Tea seemed to be over far too soon.

Then, to my horror, I heard a member of staff say, 'Does anyone want to go back into the Wacky Warehouse to play?'

What? Was she for real? I thought we'd done that bit. Understandably, the question got cheers all round from the children. Twenty minutes left. No, no, please, no more. I kept willing it to be over; I was mortified. But it was too late: they were already charging past me at speed, like a herd of cattle, back off to play ... and this time they had the added bonus of the E-numbers they'd just eaten and drank for their tea to whizz them up a little bit more.

I put the 'Rottweiler' back on the door and hoped for the best whilst I paced around the play gym on patrol, just waiting for six o'clock to arrive. It couldn't come soon enough for me. There were one or two more disagreements to sort out. We had a little nosebleed, a squashed finger and a knee injury, but then, at last, the first parent arrived.

I've never been so pleased to see her; I almost gave her a kiss. I was very pleased I didn't, however, as this was only the second time I'd met her so it may have seemed a little forward. Then slowly, one by one, they arrived to pick up their little darlings, looking really chilled after their two hours of freedom.

'Has it all gone okay?' one dad asked me.

'Yes smashing, loved it,' I lied.

As the last one left, my mum and I flopped down, exhausted. 'You said this was an easier way of doing parties. I'm not so sure,' she said. 'No, neither am I. Are you coming back to mine for a glass of wine?' My mother doesn't drink, but I wanted to offer.

'Yes please' was her very quick reply.

Once home, I handed her a bottle of wine with a straw in it. She looked at me, puzzled. 'That's yours,' I said. 'I've got mine here!'

Being left a little bruised from this experience, we then worked our way through quite a huge range of children's party themes. Amongst many, there was a 'Doctor Who' party, where the porch became a Tardis, with home-made daleks and monsters all around our house. Halloween parties have always gone down very well with both children and parents, and my house has been completely trashed on a number of occasions.

There have been kids falling asleep in their food, tears and lots of laughter. We've even had beach parties in January, and on one very cold August day we had eleven screaming thirteen-year-old girls running around the garden, all throwing water bombs at Gary – although as he was dressed in a full wetsuit, snorkel and mask this wasn't too much of a problem for him.

As well as loving organising Abbie's and James's parties, and being almost as giddy as them when the day actually arrived, we've had great fun at many of our friends' and families' parties too. At only seven months old, Tom and James attended their first fancy dress party. The pair of them looked extremely cute dressed as Laurel and Hardy, with Tom's round face and dark hair and James's thin face and light tufty hair. Despite the fact that they were barely sitting up, everyone knew exactly who they were meant to be. This was for a party which the host, Annabelle, slept the whole way through, obviously exhausted with the excitement. I think at two years old, though, when it's your party, you can get away with doing exactly what you want to do. Poor Ellen, her mum, had spent months organising it. All was not lost, though, as a great time was had by all the rest of her guests.

Party Bags

I feel I must just mention this little fad. I'm not even sure if these are still as popular as they used to be, but certainly when Abbie was younger, the party bag was almost as important as the party itself. Such a clever idea somebody came up with where not only do you provide a party, feed everyone's kids and give their parents two hours of freedom, but you're then expected to fill a little plastic bag with sweets and small toys to send home with every child. I can remember only too well dashing out an hour or so before everyone was due to arrive at our parties, all because I felt I hadn't put enough stuff in them – always to Gary's dismay.

'They're coming to the party, not for a bag. It's all going to get thrown away as soon as they get home,' he would shout at me as I ran towards the car, nipping off to the supermarket, in a panic. 'It's a load of twaddle!'

I knew he was right, but I just couldn't stop myself as I'd suddenly remembered some of the great things that had been in the bags Abbie had come home with. I didn't want the other mums thinking that I was a cheapskate.

How silly that all seems now. But I can tell you at the time it really did feel that important. We talk about peer pressure in school for our children. Well, those party bags can – and did – put us mums under some pressure. It only took one mum to up the ante with the gifts and that was it: everyone else would follow suit. Looking back, I know that most of the parents wouldn't have noticed what was in them. Even if they'd been in the slightest bit interested, the kids would have most likely eaten everything in the bag way before they arrived home, no doubt losing or throwing the toys away in the process. Does it really matter? After all, it's the thought that counts.

Birthday Cakes

Many years ago, back in 1994 as Abbie's first birthday approached, I came up with the bright idea of baking her a cake. It was an impressive cake – one I'd spent a great deal of time on – but when I say impressive, I only mean in size as the intricate design I'd worked on throughout the night looked nothing like a duck in a pond.

This was the start of the birthday cake tradition – a tradition that, twenty-two years on, is still happening. It's bad enough that people have to put up with my cakes on birthdays, but it doesn't stop at that: the Halloween cake I once made for our party managed to confuse all the guests. Everyone seemed to think I'd decorated it with a picture of the dog on the top when I'd actually attempted to do a scary ghostly scene. I guess the black and white icing I'd made was a little over-runny, and as it all merged together on the top of the cake, I must admit it did slightly resemble a sheepdog shape. Many a time on the eve of a birthday, Gary has wandered into the kitchen well after midnight only to find me still battling on, trying desperately to get a cake finished before the morning.

'Wouldn't it just be easier, and probably cheaper, to go buy one, Jo?'

You'd think that by now, with all the practice I've had, I'd be really quite good at making them, but I'm not; they always look home-made. I've attempted to make gymnasts, teddy bears, hedgehogs, football pitches and swimming pools, amongst many other things. Some look quite good but taste dreadful, whilst others look rubbish but taste quite nice. I just never seem to get it all right at the same time. In fact, the last cake I made for James was probably my worst effort yet ...

On the eve of James's fourteenth birthday, I'd gone shopping to buy all my usual ingredients for his cake. Whilst walking down the aisle and seeing all the beautifully made cakes, I thought to myself, shall I just buy one? It's already late and they do look lovely. Then proceeded the start of a little tennis match in my brain where I'd convince myself that was a great idea, put one of the beautifully decorated Doctor Who cakes in my trolley, only to then, two minutes later, go put it back on the shelf again. Having done this several times, and noticing the store manager looking at me in a suspicious way, I then realised I'd been stuck at deuce in my tennis match for a good fifteen minutes now and I really didn't have the time for this. I put the cake back down for the fifth and final time. No, I'd never missed a birthday yet and I wasn't going to let James down. So I continued, as planned, to buy all the ingredients I needed for the chocolate orange cake I'd seen in a recipe book earlier that day.

All seemed to be going very well at first. The chocolate and orange smelt lovely as I mixed together all the ingredients. It wasn't until I came to put it into the baking tin that I became a little concerned. The recipe said to pour the mixture into the tin. My mixture was so thick that I was struggling to even stir it – there was no way it was going to pour anywhere. In fact, I wasn't sure how I was going to get it out of the bowl. Eventually, after some pretty heavy scraping, it started to leave the side of the bowl then plopped into the baking tin in one great big lump. At this point I could only hope that the heat of the oven would soften it somewhat and that maybe it might come out a much better shape than it had gone in!

Unfortunately for me, it didn't. It was, even after forty minutes' cooking, exactly the same shape it had been before it'd gone in. It certainly didn't look like a cake and, just to make things worse, I then noticed the grated orange peel on the plate at the side of the oven. Oh dear, that was meant to be inside the cake. Not one to be defeated, I put the cake on a plate, popped it on the table and sprinkled the orange peel on the top, leaving it there to show James when he got home from school! On returning home that afternoon he seemed highly amused. 'Well, Mum, I think that's your best effort yet.' Pausing for a minute, he then bravely cut himself a slab.

'I think it might be better with a bit of custard on,' he said with a mouth full of cake.

'No, love, bless you for trying, but I think the bin's the only thing that would help.'

At this point Abbie returned home. 'What an earth is that?' she screeched.

After we'd all finally stopped laughing and calmed down, I decided I was going to bite the bullet, go back to the supermarket to buy that cake I'd been admiring the previous evening. But Abbie had other ideas: she was adamant she was going to make him another one. To be fair, she'd started doing a bit of baking and was getting quite good at it, so I happily left her to it. Two hours later she produced a beautiful, moist chocolate cake that looked amazing.

Would this be the end of my baking career? Sadly not.

Words of Wisdom

Can I guide you in any way to a successful party? Only to tell you to expect the unexpected. I don't think there's a wrong or a right way to do them. It's all down to how it pans out on the day because even the best laid plans can go belly-up. I'm still learning, and we've now moved on to parties involving alcohol, which is a whole new ball game – perhaps for another book.

As for making your own birthday cakes, I'd say never give up … although I imagine my family and friends might tell you different.

Beware of the party bag, if they're still out there. I do hate to admit it, but Gary was right: 'They're a load of twaddle!'

21

Relax, I'm in control

Holidaying with family or friends is a great idea. You can help each other out with childcare, ensuring that you each get a little break from parenting. The children can all play together whilst the adults sit and enjoy the luxury of sunbathing. That's the theory anyway.

We went away with my brother, wife Sue and their daughter whilst the children were still young. Their daughter, Rose, was four, and my two were nine and eighteen months old.

Abbie, on her first day swimming, found a euro on the bottom of the pool, after which we saw very little of her as she then spent the rest of the holiday under the water, searching for more money. She did make friends with plenty of other children her age, and they too seemed happy to spend their holiday under the water looking for euros, so Abbie was content and more than happy with her little group of like-minded friends.

James, at this stage, was still needing a little nap in the afternoons; this re-charged his batteries, enabling him to stop up late and party with the rest us of an evening. Gary and Steven saw this as a good opportunity to earn themselves some brownie points, as each afternoon the moment James started to show any signs that he needed a sleep, they would get him straight into his pram and whisk him off for a walk. How lovely and thoughtful of them. This, of course, had nothing to do with the World Cup being in full swing at this time. I do believe each afternoon involved a visit to the pub, with James fast asleep. The two of them could enjoy a nice pint whilst they caught up on the football. They were often gone for a few hours, or at least until James woke up. I think it would then be a case of how much pop and crisps they could feed James to keep him happy in his pram until eventually he'd want out, leaving them with no choice but to return back to the pool.

Whilst they were away, Sue and I would take it in turns to watch the girls. This gave each of us in turn a nice relaxing sunbathe for an hour – a real treat for us both. Abbie was more than happy with her friends and apart from re-applying her sun cream and throwing her a bit of food from time to time there wasn't much else she needed. Rose, on the other hand, being only four, did take a little more looking after. As she was renowned for her clumsiness, it was just best to never leave her side at all. So, when it was my turn to be on watch, that's exactly what I did.

On this particular day, when it was my stint, Rose and I were playing catch in the small baby pool. She wasn't quite off swimming just yet, but she didn't have her armbands on as the water was only knee-deep. It was another beautiful day and with the sun shining in my eyes I needed to wear my sunglasses so I could see the ball when it was coming my way. We were playing merrily for a good half hour and Rose was improving her catching skills at an alarming rate. Then, suddenly, she threw the ball a little bit too far and it went over into the big pool. As Rose was just next to the steps, she automatically started running towards them as she fully intended to climb out and jump into the big pool to get our ball back. I was at the other side so I started to run as quickly as I could to get to her, shouting, 'Rose! No! Come here, I'll get it.'

There was so much noise going on in the pool area she couldn't hear me shouting – either that or she had chosen to ignore me. So I continued trying my best to run after her.

This wasn't at all easy through the water, as I was getting nowhere fast. In fact it felt like I was running in slow motion, and by now she was already out of our pool and running down the steps into the big pool.

'Rose! No! You haven't got your armbands on!' I shouted in a panic.

Still not being able to hear me, she just jumped straight in after the ball. I clambered up the steps as fast as I could, then just launched myself down the other steps into the big pool. I couldn't see her as she had gone under the water, but I knew she couldn't be far as she was only seconds in front of me. I too went under the water – it was deeper than I'd anticipated. I popped back up: still no sign of her. Grabbing a breath and going back under the water, panic-stricken, I was desperately fumbling around under the water, hoping to feel or see her. Running out of breath, I had to come back up for a third time. Then I spotted something just to the left of where I'd been looking. Diving back down, at last I felt something. I just grabbed and tried with all my strength to drag her upwards. Still not able to stand up myself, I pulled her head out of the water, desperately trying to remember what I'd learnt at school during life-saving. I flipped her over on to her back and then we swam and sank a bit until at last I felt the bottom step. I dragged her and myself up on to the next few steps, getting us both out of the water. Turning her over, I could see then she was breathing, as she was coughing and spluttering. I started rubbing and patting her back to help her get rid of some of the water she'd taken in. My heart was pounding, but I was so relieved. We both just collapsed on the steps, looking like a couple of drowned rats. Her usually big curly hair was pinned flat to her head, her face extremely pale, but she was alive.

What had just happened there? One minute we were having a great time, then the next I was living a nightmare. It was at this point I realised my sunglasses had amazingly managed to stay on my face – albeit they were only over the one eye now, and the other side was hanging down and dangling off the edge of my nose. By now we'd gathered a small audience as a few people had come over to see if we were okay.

'Yes, thanks, we are now. Rose just forgot for a minute that she couldn't swim!' I told them, as a load of water came flooding down my nose. 'Did you forget you didn't have your armbands on, Rose darling?' My heart was still beating so fast and as I looked at little Rose sat there on the steps, I suddenly wanted to cry.

Thank goodness Sue was still flat out on her sunbed and had seen none of what had just happened. Why me? And with someone else's child? We sat for a while, dazed, I think. Tears were rolling down my face.

'Why are you crying, Auntie Jojo?' she asked me, seeming quite confused.

'Don't you ever do that again, Rose. You frightened me to death. I thought we'd lost you.'

Amazingly, she didn't seem too perturbed by what had just happened; in fact, shortly after, she asked if she could have an ice cream. Astonished at her resilience, but extremely pleased to see that she was absolutely fine, I agreed it was a good idea. Besides, I certainly didn't feel ready to wake her mum up right now. So, I took the opportunity to get both her and Abbie an ice cream, whilst I had a rather large brandy.

When it came to explaining it to her mum? Well, I played it down just a little. It wasn't until much later that evening, after quite a few drinks, that the full tale actually came out.

Words of Wisdom

When in the vicinity of a pool, armbands at all times, I think. Not quite making five foot myself, that goes for me too.

It just goes to show when put in an emergency situation you'll pretty much do anything. Until that afternoon I'd only ever dipped my toe in the big pool, which had confirmed to me it was far too cold in there for my liking, and under no circumstances would I be going in.

22

Always wear sunscreen

Sun cream, for my family, has always been a tough one. As I mentioned earlier my skin in winter is slightly blue, possibly changing to a white shade in spring – not the kind that particularly likes the sun. Regardless of this, I did try very hard to achieve the perfect suntan that all my olive-skinned friends seemed to have. Alas, it became clear after years of red, sore and often quiet painful nights in bed that for me, this wasn't to be. With this in mind, when my own children came along I realised it was quite possible that they too would need to be very cautious where the sun was concerned. Luckily for them, the human race was by now fully aware of the damage the sun can do to your skin. It was no longer cool and trendy to sit out baking in the sunshine for hours. People's attitudes towards the sun had changed dramatically, and sun creams were far more advanced. Anybody caught going out in the sun wearing just oil, as was completely acceptable in my dad's day, would now have been considered insane.

Abbie, being the eldest by six years, was very much the guinea pig and spent the first five years of her life trailing multiple brands and factors of sun cream. The higher the factor, so we thought, the better for her with her delicate skin. This system does come with its own complications, because the higher the factor, the thicker the cream, making it almost impossible to rub in. Now, little ones don't tend to like standing still for any amount of time, especially when they can see a beach or swimming pool within their sights. You may get away with it on the first exciting morning on holiday, but once they get to know what's coming, they aren't going to cooperate at all. Abbie certainly didn't, especially with the added bonus of my ice-cold hands, resulting in a then moving target. On the plus side, though, if you did get broken off in the middle of applying it, there was never any doubt as to where you'd got to – the thick, white consistency left a clear indication of any bits still left to do. Eventually, when this small mission had been accomplished, it was then down to the beach with my shiny white child, now verging on luminous, who would then very quickly become a human magnet for sand, becoming almost unrecognisable within minutes.

As if her pale complexion wasn't enough to contend with on holiday, Abbie also seemed to have an allergic reaction to certain sun creams. Some made her go blotchy, with red patches in random places, whilst others didn't seem to protect her at all. It seemed no matter what we tried there wasn't anything that ticked all the boxes for her. Each time she stepped out of the sea or pool on holiday I would reapply more as I was scared she would get sunburnt. It's pretty much an impossible task to put cream on at the beach without just a little bit of sand sticking to your hands; this generally meant that as well as more sun cream Abbie would also get fully exfoliated. I'm not overly sure this was what her delicate skin really needed. No surprise, then, that she had a love—hate relationship with the sun, sea and the sand. Interestingly enough, her first encounter with the sand surprised us very much – it wasn't what we were expecting at all. She was about ten months old. Sitting her on the towel as we got to the beach that morning, we fully expected her to run off, but to our surprise she just sat there. After a while, as Gary was eager to start building sand castles with her, he eventually picked her up and carried her on to the sand. However, as he lowered her down and her toes touched the sand, she immediately curled her feet up as far underneath her as she could.

'Ey, watch this, Jo!' he shouted up to me.

Each time he put her near the sand, she panicked as her feet touched it, retracting her legs up underneath her as far away from the sand as she could. This was quite hilarious to watch, but eventually she did start to cry, so we sat her back down on the towel, where she was more than happy. This is where she stayed – for the whole day, so it proved to be a very easy day at the beach for us.

A trip to visit my sister in Australia in 1999 was where we were introduced to an ingenious piece of clothing – a sunsuit. This was the best thing we ever found for Abbie, making life a lot easier. Cream now only need to be applied to her face and the bottom of her arms and legs. Just to be sure, we also put her a peeked cap on with material to cover the back of her neck, meaning that she was undoubtedly now pretty well covered. She was the only child on the flight home from Australia that was actually paler than she'd been on the way there. If I'm honest I would have liked her to have just had a little bit of colour after her holidays, but it wasn't to be. The sunsuit did serve her well for a good few years. Inevitably, there did come a day when she refused to wear it. Understandably, she wanted to wear pretty bikinis like the rest of the girls. It was then back to experimenting with different sun creams once more.

Spending most of her holidays under the water didn't help matters much, as constantly wearing goggles would make the skin under her eyes quite red. That – added to the chlorine in the swimming pool, or the salt in the sea, mixed together with sun cream and sunshine – meant that by the end of each day, her cheekbones and just under her eyes were absolutely raw. The skin was often so red and sore that showering on an evening was no fun for her – in fact, it was more like torture. I feel sure the people in the apartments around us must have thought we were killing her because as soon as the water from the shower touched her cheeks she would scream the place down. As for trying to put a little aftersun on for her, this would involve chasing her around the apartment once more, as while it helped calm the skin down eventually, it did sting initially. Going out each evening with her, I'll admit I did feel a little embarrassed. I would notice the odd person staring; I'm almost sure they were thinking I hadn't put any sun cream on my child. I did contemplate sticking a notice on her saying, 'I'm not burnt, it's an allergic reaction'! As amazingly as it had arrived, by the next morning the redness had always gone, her eyes were back to normal, and she would be fine, and straight back into the pool. The whole of the previous evening's performance was forgotten and she was up for doing it all again. So the entire process would start once more.

Words of Wisdom

There's nothing wrong with pale skin, although it's taken me a long time to get my head round that one. It's actually now very fashionable. But if you have a problem with that there's always the fake tan route, which, like sun cream, has improved immensely over the years. Not that I'm recommending putting it on your children, of course. That would be a ridiculous idea ... or would it?

I imagine most children can stand a little sunshine, but if yours have skin as delicate as mine do maybe you should think about holidaying in England; that way you can more or less guarantee they'll be quite safe from the sun.

If, like me, you suffer with cold hands all year round, I'd strongly advise you to use this excuse and opportunity and sit back for a little while. Enjoy watching someone else chase the kids around trying to get their sun cream on.

23

Hannibal Lecter

Biting your best friend is perhaps not something you want to get into the habit of doing, but I'm afraid that was exactly what James did. Fortunately for me, his best friend's mum was my best friend.

It started in July, out in the garden, over a disagreement with a Little Tikes pedal car. Both boys wanted to play with it at the same time and after a tug of war session, some hard stares and a good few tears, James bit Tom on the arm. Now, Tom usually won the battle-of-wills contests between them both as he was, shall we say, slightly smarter than James. Nevertheless, it seemed, at this point, all those months of pure frustration had finally got the better of James because as he sank his teeth into Tom's arm an amazing thing happened: Tom not only let go of the car but he also ran away, leaving James quite stunned for a minute, probably wondering where Tom had gone and why. He then quickly jumped into the car, which was now his, realising finally he'd found a way to get the better of Tom. I'm afraid to say this was then the start of many an assault on poor Tom.

Over the years I've spoken to mums who have been devastated because their little one had started biting. Well, it's not that bad, I'd thought, but realised then that it is. It's not nice at all. I would much rather Tom had been the one biting James; as the mother of a biter, it has you living in fear as to when, where and who they're going to bite next.

Unfortunately for Tom, it did only seem to be him that James would bite, and I have to say that he was very brave throughout it all. One evening, whilst Stacey was undressing him for bed, she took his vest off and noticed teeth marks on his chest. Now, being that she'd been looking after James for me that day, the odds are she knew who'd done it but just didn't know why or when it had happened, because Tom hadn't come crying to Stacey at any point throughout that day. It was a perfect mouth-shaped mark on Tom's chest, and I feel sure that if we'd got forensic in and measured James's mouth span, it would have been a perfect match.

One day Stacey had left Tom with me for the afternoon as she was at the hospital with her second child, Hannah, who was only weeks old. She'd been born with a serious bowel disorder, so poor Stacey had rather a lot on her plate once more, and I was trying to help as best I could by having Tom stay with us. This was when James bit Tom on the cheek whilst they were playing 'Pinch the Dummy' – another pure frustration moment for James I think. Tom had pinched his dummy one too many times that day and was refusing to give it back – not that that makes it okay, of course. Once again, James went in with his teeth – only this time it was Tom's cheek he went for, more than likely because Tom was sat with both dummies in his mouth.

'No! No, James!' I shouted, but it was too late, the damage was done: it started to bleed.

I'm not great with blood and unfortunately there did seem to be plenty of it. I started to panic: It's going to need stitches. What an earth am I going to tell Stacey? He's going to be scarred for life. As if she needs this! I was distraught. Up to now, Stacey had always been really good about it, usually saying Tom deserved biting for winding James up. With everything else she had going on I felt sure it would be the end of our friendship. Poor Tom – tears rolled down his little cheeks, which wasn't helping matters as the more he cried the more he bled, and the tears mixed with the blood made him look like he'd met a mad axeman; he was in a real mess. Please don't let Stacey walk in now. I was trying my best to stop the bleeding, which wasn't easy as Tom was so upset. James, at this point, had now piped up and started to cry along with Tom.

'You're just going to have to sit there, James. There's nothing wrong with you. Look at the mess you've made of Tom!'

It was chaos. I felt dreadful. After some time, which felt like forever, I did manage to calm him down and stop the bleeding. Thankfully, it didn't look quite as bad as I'd first thought. It still wasn't good though, was it? I sat James on the naughty step and gave Tom some sweets. I was feeling positively sick by the time Stacey returned. After listening to her telling me all about what was happening to little Hanna, I then had to explain what had happened to Tom.

'It's his own fault, then. He knows how much James loves his dummy. He would have probably done the same, roles reversed' was her quick reply.

'Don't you want to bite James, or hit me, or anything?' I asked her, quite puzzled.

Once again, she'd been more than good about it, as I'm sure this is something that mums could quite easily fall out over. As great as she'd been, I still felt awful, and James just seemed to be getting worse with this biting thing. What was I going to do with him? What if he does this when he starts school? Surely he won't still be doing it then, will he? I just couldn't see an end to it. To me, kids will play and fall out, and pushing, arguing, even punching, are all perfectly acceptable things for your toddlers to do, but biting, really? That's not normal in my book. Stacey really had been pretty cool about the whole thing and I'm sure roles reversed I would have been fine with Tom biting James – in fact, I would have preferred it. I worried there was something wrong with him to make him even do this in the first place. Abbie had never bitten anyone. More advice, of course, came flooding in.

'Bite him back, see how he likes it.'

Surely it's not right to bite your own children, is it? As much as I was at my wits' end I just couldn't bring myself to do that. We went through the usual punishments, sat him on the naughty step, sent him up to his room and took his favourite toys away from him.

Then, funnily enough, one day about three months later I suddenly had a thought: James hasn't bitten Tom for ages ... I wonder if he's finally stopped doing that.

Well, I'm still wondering, and it's been a good few years now.

Words of Wisdom

Just a phase he was going through, I hear you say. A phase indeed – one of the many that come from nowhere, often to then vanish into thin air as if they've never happened, but not without causing a significant amount of heartache first.

If you too have a biter, what can I tell you to try and help? I could tell you not to worry and to just ride it out, but I know for sure under these circumstances that's easier said than done. I don't think human muzzles are available on the NHS, but it might be worth looking into. Perhaps there's an opening in the market there for someone, because if I had come across one back then, without a shadow of a doubt, I'd have definitely given it a try.

24

Come fly with me

Children, especially babies, can make flying very stressful. It's always a worry as to how you're going to keep them occupied and quiet in view of the fact that once they get bored or frustrated there's just nowhere to go with them. Now, once the plane's airborne, you have the chance to get out of your seat and pace up and down the aisle. This, I feel, only annoys everyone else on the flight, as well as the poor people having to sit next to you and your fidgety children. We all know there is no chance they're going to be happy sat still on your knee or in their own seats for the whole journey. All you can do is hope and pray that the people sat around you either have children, or have had children at some point and will understand what you're going through.

It can be even harder with the very young ones as babies can't even tell you what's wrong with them. If they start to cry it's pretty much a guessing game as to why. Are they in any pain, or is it that they're just fed up with themselves? The answer: you may never know. Perhaps a spoonful of Calpol before you fly might help, just in case their ears are effected by the altitude. I mean, even if they're not in any pain, it would help to make them more relaxed and maybe sleep for a little while, but then I'm not sure if that would be classed as drugging them. What if they're sick over everyone, or in need of a nappy change and they stink the whole plane out? It's such a small, confined area there's nowhere to hide. All these things, and many more, will perhaps be going through your mind before you fly. But when you yourself aren't the best on airplanes – or, even worse, are extremely frightened of flying – it really is a recipe for fun and games.

Not renowned for being the most confident of flyers myself, I have to try desperately hard to act calm in these situations, if nothing else then for the sake of my children. For me, this isn't always easy, especially when my heart's beating ten times faster than it usually does and I can't string a proper sentence together, probably because I've had to take a Valium or two to get me anywhere near the airport in the first place, never mind on to the plane.

So, as my youngest's holding on to my very clammy shaking hand whilst boarding the aircraft and saying to me, 'Come on, Mummy. It's going to be alright, don't be scared', I kind of know I haven't quite managed to fool him – or anybody else, for that matter.

I'd say this combination could play havoc with your head and possibly contribute to saying and doing some rather strange things. This taken into account, Gary always takes control at airports. He knows only too well by now that the only stuff that comes out of my mouth in such situations is usually rubbish and makes very little sense. So as we went through security at Manchester Airport when James was only three, we were all a little surprised when the security guard held up James's hand luggage

'Who's bag is this, please?'

Gary walked over to the very serious looking men.

'There's a gun inside this bag, sir.'

'What!!' Gary looked very confused.

'Did you pack this bag, sir?'

'Oh, no, it was my wife. It's my son's bag. Of course, it's only a plastic gun, though,' Gary said with a little smile.

'I don't know whether it's plastic or real do I, sir? On the screen, it looks like a gun to me!' the red-faced security guard answered. He wasn't impressed; in fact, he was getting more serious by the second. At this point I noticed quite a lot more security guards and a couple of policemen gathering round. No one else seemed to be using our conveyer belt any more; they were all being diverted somewhere else.

'Oh, yes, sorry, it was me. I put that in there just before we left home this morning, and actually I think there's a hand grenade in there too. They were really light, you see, so I thought they'd be great for keeping him occupied on the plane.'

I rambled on and on and on until eventually I could feel Gary's stare burning into the side of my head. I looked over at him and he was shaking his head, so I stopped mid-sentence and stared at the floor. Everyone around us had now gone completely silent and they were all staring at me in astonishment. It wasn't really until that point that I realised what I'd actually done in my manic state earlier that morning, just before we'd left the house and whilst everyone else was waiting for me in the car. I was dashing around doing all the usual stuff us mums do before going on holiday: putting some bleach down the toilet, checking I'd emptied the bins and the fridge. Then I saw them – they were just there, left out on the floor and I thought, oh they're nice and light for James's hand luggage, he can play with them on holiday. So I popped them into his little bag.

Thought it was a great idea … until this point.

They then proceeded to empty the whole bag out on to the table. Yes, I was right, the hand grenade was in there too. The security guard wasn't impressed; neither were the police officers – in fact, they all looked pretty serious right now. I'm not really sure if they were so cross because they'd missed finding the hand grenade in the first place or just because they couldn't believe anyone could be so stupid as to put it in there. Either way, I wasn't their favourite person.

'Had you been travelling to America, we wouldn't have let you on the plane. You would have been sent straight home.'

Oh dear, it's a shame I wasn't, as right now I really did want to go home. I'd already had enough. I hadn't even seen the plane yet and I think my Valium had all but worn off. Now, just to add to my nausea, racing heart, shaking and clammy hands, I was very close to being arrested. Completely bright red and very hot, I examined my feet intensely. I dared not look at Gary, or James, come to think of it. The rest of the family we were travelling with seemed to have made themselves scarce. I was really hoping they had Abbie with them as with all the palaver I'd only just realised she wasn't about. We kind of knew they weren't going to let us keep James's toys.

'You can pick these up when you return to England,' the security guard told us as he glared at me.

So, with that, we scurried off, as fast as we possibly could, hoping never to see any of these people, ever again. James was just about to break into a small tantrum, wanting to know why his toys had been taken away from his bag. I had no answer as my verbal diarrhoea seemed to have completely dried up. Gary explained to James that the man had liked the toys so much, he'd asked if they could play with them, just while we were away on our holidays.

Amazingly, and to our surprise, he took that pretty well. 'Can I have them back when we come home, Daddy?'

'Yes, 'course you can,' Gary reassured him.

I personally hoped after two weeks away he might have forgotten all about them. I suppose if you look for something good coming out of the whole experience, at least it'd taken my mind off flying for a little while. Gary just kept looking at me and shaking his head in amusement and disbelief. I don't think he could be too cross with me as he knew in his heart of hearts that this would be one of those little things that we'd laugh about for years to come.

Incidentally, on returning to England two weeks later, just as the wheels touched down on the runway, a certain small boy shouted out, 'Daddy, can we go and get my gun back now?'

Words of Wisdom

To my fellow nervous flyers: if you haven't thought about packing them before departure day, it doesn't matter how light and plastic they are – just leave them at home.

I'm not sure it's babies you need to be too worried about on planes. Maybe nervous flyers shouldn't be left to their own devices up to twenty-four hours prior to take off – especially when Valium's involved.

25

As easy as riding a bike

It's one of those big moments in every child's life; exciting, nerve-racking and often quite emotional. For our two children, though, there couldn't have been two more different experiences.

Back in September 1996, when Abbie was three, Gary had spent a lot of his time that summer, mainly evenings, with her at Harewood House. It was a local manor house with fantastic gardens, big open spaces for picnicking, adventure playgrounds and a small animal area. I always worked late on Thursday and Friday evenings so he'd take Abbie there as she loved it; they'd often be gone for hours. After visiting there many a time and having to pay £9 to go in, he then realised that for £20 you could get a year's membership. Without further ado he signed up for that, and consequently I didn't see very much of the pair of them for the rest of the summer. It had a lovely big penguin enclosure, and I understand she knew each penguin by name. With all kinds of birds there, and a huge play area, it really was a lovely place for her be. I actually do believe she thought she lived there and that it was all her very own garden. As Gary had now started to take her bike along with them, she was getting plenty of practice and doing very well. In fact, he reckoned she'd soon have the stabilisers off because Abbie was so determined and very independent – two qualities that turned out to be extremely helpful.

Only a month later, Gary came home very pleased with himself. 'She's done it – she's on two wheels. We won't be needing these stabilisers anymore!' he shouted extremely proudly as they both rushed in through the salon door.

There was a cheer from all the staff and customers who were in that evening. What an achievement! She was only three, and so tiny. She looked too small to be riding a bike – but she was. That determination and independence had served her well. What an idyllic, lovely experience it had been all round, and Abbie was now riding a bike at a very early age, looking very pleased and proud of herself as she walked through the salon, strutting past everyone like she was Lady Harewood herself.

Quickly moving on a few years to 2005 … This particular morning we were all walking down to the park, 'all' being my sister, Abbie, James and me (Gary was at work). It was a lovely morning and quite warm for April. The dog needed a walk and James was pestering to take his bike with us. He'd finally got going on two wheels.

As James was now five, Gary had been eager to get him started. 'Abbie was only three and she was riding a bike. James really needs to get going now.'

They'd been going to practise at the skate park for a good few weeks now, and the stabilisers were finally off. Today he wanted to show Aunty Helen and me how he could ride his bike without them. While we were watching him ride around the skate park, my brother phoned to say that he was near our house and was thinking of calling in. I explained to him we were in the park and to meet us at the café near the bottom entrance. He was obviously nearer than I thought because not too long after putting the phone down he called back to say he'd arrived at the café. After calling James and trying to get his attention for quite some time, he eventually responded, but looked rather fed up as he obviously didn't want to stop riding his bike just yet. He asked if he could ride it down to the café.

'Yes, go on then, but nice and slow, go steady.'

When I looked up from fastening the dog's lead I could see James just reaching the top of the hill. 'Slowly, James! Use your brakes!' I shouted.

I could see he'd just set off, and he did seem to be gathering speed. He was on the path leading down towards the café, which did get rather steep as you approached the outside seating area. I started to run after him, knowing full well I wasn't going to be able to get anywhere near him. It was just mother's instinct, I think.

I could feel myself getting faster and faster shouting, 'Use the brakes, James! Slow down!'

It was useless, as he was by now too far away from me to be able to hear my shouting, and gathering more speed by the second. In my efforts to try and stop him I just kept running with the dog on the lead, who thought this was a great game – he wasn't used to me running this fast. I ran past people who were looking and pointing in James's direction. I knew Steven was going to be at the café, but there was no time to try and ring him – it was all happening so fast. Knowing full well that when James reached the café he was going to have to stop somewhere as the path ended there. Oh no, he's never going to hold it together when he flies off the kerb edge. Should he manage to stay on after the kerb then there's an open area there which will be full of people queuing up for ice creams. Please let someone catch him – provided he doesn't run them over first, that is.

I was in a real panic, still running but feeling completely powerless. When he finally did reach the kerb edge, still apparently having no way off stopping, he amazingly did stay on the bike – I have no idea how – but he was now heading towards the café at tremendous speed. Managing to miss every person in the ice cream queue, his only way of stopping now was the side of the café ... which is exactly what he did. There was a huge 'thud' and his bike finally came to a standstill as James flew off into the wall. Steven and his family just watched in amazement and horror, as there was absolutely nothing that they could have done. It had all happened in a flash and, to be fair to them, they didn't even know James was on his way. I feel sure at the speed he was travelling all they'd have seen of him was a blur.

When I finally caught up with him, puffing and panting with a very excited dog that thought this was a great game, Steven had James in his arms, and a lot of people had gathered around him. I came rushing up to them, my heart thumping so hard, not knowing what kind of a state James was going to be in.

'James! James! Is he okay?'

He was conscious, which was unbelievable, really, judging by the size of what can only be described as a very large egg on his forehead. He had, of course, been wearing his helmet, but it must have been blown back from his forehead as he'd picked up so much speed! His poor little head had gone straight into the side of the café – although had the café not been there, the next stop would have been the river. I'm not really too sure which would have been worse.

He was extremely pale. The lady from the café had brought out an ice pack, which was very much appreciated. As we were trying to gently press it on to his head, he kept pushing it away, obviously in quite a lot of pain. Eventually he let me hold the ice on it for a little while; I felt relieved about this as he was refusing to go to the hospital and would only stop crying when I promised that I wouldn't take him there. Holding him in my arms, I couldn't tell who was shaking more: him or me. He'd frightened the life out of a lot of people in the park that morning, and some kept coming over to see if he was okay.

They'd seen him flying past them earlier, shortly followed by me screaming, 'Use your brakes, James!' After some time we did manage to calm him down, and an ice cream seemed to help, until someone mentioned going to the hospital again, and then the tears would start up. He was adamant he wasn't going. Steven kept looking at James and shaking his head.

'I'm so sorry, there was nothing I could do.'

'Why didn't you use your brakes, James?' I eventually asked him.

'I don't know how to do brakes' was his reply, through his sobbing.

'What?!'

Then it suddenly hit me: all the times he'd been with Gary to practise, they'd only ridden around the skate park. The skate park which was completely flat, so it would appear they hadn't got round to using the brakes just yet. Poor James – it looked like the cause of the accident was a bit of missed communication between Gary and me. I felt dreadful.

I kept my eye on James that day and night and did try, on numerous occasions, to convince him that a trip to the hospital would be fun. He was having none of it. Fortunately, all appeared fine with him. He did have quite an impressive bruise, which over the next week or so changed colour nearly every day. I did question myself constantly over the next few weeks, regretting not taking him to the hospital. Perhaps I should have insisted he went. However, it only seemed to upset him – just mention hospitals and he would burst into tears. I felt he'd be much better sitting calmly at home with me.

Words of Wisdom

Could there be two more different experiences? I think not.

From the calm, tranquil grounds of Harewood House, and a tiny little girl merrily riding along effortlessly with her dad, to the manic, out-of-control little boy, travelling at speed through a busy park with – as we now know – clearly no knowledge of where or how to use his brakes.

A small tip here: if, like us, you work opposing shifts and bike practice is being shared amongst you both, perhaps then it might be a good idea to jot down some information for each other on shift change to ensure small details such as 'he hasn't learnt to use the brakes yet' don't get overlooked.

26

Furry friends

Pets. Like children, try as you may to put it off, they're probably something that you're going to have to face up to sooner or later. Feeling sorry for Abbie a few months after James had been born, I softened one day and came home with two gerbils for her. She really wanted a rabbit, but as Gary wasn't even aware we were getting a pet, I thought it best we start small. They were cute little things, and she liked them a lot. Gary wasn't impressed, so Daisy and Daffodil lived in their cage in her bedroom, out of his way.

Even though Abbie liked them a great deal, this didn't necessarily mean she looked after them particularly well. In fact, the smell in her room on occasions was pretty bad, and as I didn't want Gary saying 'I told you so', I regularly ended up cleaning out their cage for her. I also seem to remember being the only one who fed and watered them. They lived the usual eighteen months or so, and that was that.

After the gerbils left to go to a better place, it wasn't long before questions were being asked about getting a rabbit. I maybe lasted around six months before eventually I cracked under the pressure. Although Gary still hadn't agreed to this, I felt it was time, so one Sunday, whilst he was at work, I took Abbie and James to choose a rabbit.

Smudge, a beautiful white and grey floppy-eared rabbit came to live with us in September. Sadly, his time with us was to be short as only six months later he died very suddenly. As for what happened to him we shall never know, but it left poor Abbie devastated.

The ultimate pet has got to be a dog. All children want a dog, and although my two had been asking for one for years I don't think they truly believed it would ever happen. The gerbils and the rabbit were both deterrents, really, to try and divert them from constantly asking for a dog. But after Smudge's unexpected departure the pressure was on once more.

I'd been lucky enough to have a dog when I was growing up. I'd nagged my parents to death for around nine years or so, eventually wearing them down. I'd almost given up hope; then, one day, I returned home from school to find the most beautiful little puppy – she was all curled up on the rug in the front room. A dream come true for me, it was a day I'll never forget.

So when Abbie started to ask if we could have a dog when she was just a little girl, I was quite pleased, as I would have liked nothing more. However, Gary and I did not see eye to eye on this subject. Never having had pets at home when he was growing up, I don't think he really got it; he just couldn't see the point in them. We all tried to convince him it was a great idea. We lived so near to a lovely park and I only worked part-time hours, so it would never have to be left home alone for too long. There were lots of dogs in our neighbourhood. Everyone seemed to have one – everyone except us.

'It's a great way to get the kids out walking, and you love going for long walks,' I constantly told him.

I couldn't understand him at all, but he was adamant: we weren't having one, and that was that. Now, I know as parents you should always stand together with your decisions, but this time he was so wrong and I wasn't going to back down. After searching many dog rescue shelters and realising we couldn't take on an older dog that needed re-homing because our children were too young, I then started to look at puppies. There were plenty of them at the rescue centres, the only problem being that they didn't always know what kind of dog the parents had been. So it was a risk to take one on, as you were never quite sure on the breed and how big they were going to be when they were fully grown. As we'd only been living in our house for about a year we'd had all new carpets and floors fitted and it was all still looking nice and new. Now, did I really want a puppy chewing, and peeing all over, my nice new floors? What if it ate the furniture? These questions and many more I kept asking myself, as Gary wouldn't even discuss it.

'No, they're just shitting machines, all they ever do is bark. Constant barking would do my head in.'

This was all he would say on the matter. Not surprisingly then, after a few more months of 'shall we, shan't we?', Gary got his wish. I finally, but very reluctantly, gave in, as he had shown absolutely no interest whatsoever and by now I'd just about worn myself out with it all.

This would have been about May/June time, and little did we know that there was a certain collie pup just being born in the Lake District, a hundred miles or so from where we lived. He, along with his seven brothers and sisters, were born on a farm, destined for a life rounding up sheep and living outside in a barn. That was, of course, if they were one of the lucky ones, as if they were not, I'm afraid their life was to be very short, because unless the farmer could 'get rid' of them, their fate was, indeed, to be shot!

A close friend of mine, Sally, was friends with the farmer's next-door neighbours and frequently visited them with her children. Whilst on one of her visits, she heard of the fate of the puppies and promptly went round to see if she could take one home with her. Already the owner of one dog, Sally knew it might not work out, but felt it worth a try, if nothing more than to save one of those beautiful puppies from being shot.

Worried about how she was going to choose just one, and thinking she may return with all eight puppies, she went next door to have a look anyway. Thankfully, her decision was made easy by a timid little chap, who made his way from the back of the pack to come and say hello to Sally and her daughter, Jessica. His almost completely black face, with just a speck of white on his nose, immediately drew their attention to him, and then they noticed his eyes: he had the most beautiful eyes they'd ever seen. This, along with his calmness amongst all the noise and chaos going on around him, made it impossible for them to leave without him.

So it was that Jasper left the Lakes that evening and came to live in Yorkshire.

Now, he did settle down very well, with Sally's other dog, Sandy, for a good few weeks, after which she then noticed Sandy, a once confident little dog, had started to act a bit strange and was hiding under the table whilst Jasper was around. She wasn't eating and seemed threatened by the presence of a now bigger and faster dog in the house.

After giving it as long as she could and hoping that it would soon sort itself out, Sally reached the sad decision that Jasper would have to go. Having already grown to love him, it wasn't going to be easy for her and her three children to say goodbye. There really was very little not to love about him, but she couldn't possibly re-home poor Sandy, the family dog they'd had for the last four years.

Sally knew all about the battle I'd been having with Gary over the last year regarding getting a dog and wondered if I'd be interested. Well, not only was he the most handsome dog ever but he was already very obedient: he could sit, stay and lay down. He was fully potty-trained, and so far hadn't chewed or eaten anything in her house. Jasper was five months old by then, and the kids and I had met up with Sally and her children on many occasions to go for walks with the two dogs. So, as you can imagine I was more than interested as he really was perfect, our only hurdle now being Gary ...

Sally and I had a little plan: she reckoned if we could get Gary over there to see Jasper, he would definitely fall soft and wouldn't be able to resist. I sat him down that night when the kids were in bed and told him all about it.

'Please just go, have a look at him and if you don't like him then that's fine, we'll just forget about having a dog at all.' Well, maybe that was just a little white lie on my part as had he said no, I think at this point I would have acquired the dog myself and suffered the consequences ... but it was all part of the plan.

Nevertheless, he did go over to see him, as asked, and took him out for a little walk. I feel Sally did her best, showing Gary all the tricks that Jasper could do. She also explained to him that if we couldn't take him she was going to have to ring the RSPCA. Nice touch. I was, as you can imagine, still waiting up when Gary returned home that evening, far too excited and nervous to sleep. He walked in the door with a little grin on his face and I knew at that point we'd cracked him. We were getting a dog!

So a week later Jasper came to live with the Mitchells. It was a sad day for Sally and her family; it broke her heart that she had to let him go. I felt her children would hate me forever, although she was so pleased that he was coming to us and not going to the RSPCA, knowing full well they'd still see lots of him. We'd already discussed we could help each other out at holiday times – we could have Sandy for her, and she could have Jasper for us.

I was so excited and, having managed to keep all this a total secret from them, I couldn't wait to see both kids' faces when they saw him.

My dad had called around especially for the occasion. It was indeed a very exciting day. So, when they returned home from school that evening in November, Jasper was just sat there waiting calmly for them by the door.

Abbie arrived home first.

'Is this Jasper? Are we looking after him?' Abbie asked as she went to give him a cuddle.

'Yes it is, least I think so. You'd better check his collar,' I said, trying to contain myself.

She read out loud, 'Jasper Mitchell. 12 Potter Lane. What? What do you mean? Is he coming to stay with us!?'

'Yes. He's our dog now, darling. Little Sandy was getting upset with him, so he needed a new home and Sally asked me if we'd be able to have him.'

Tears started to trickle down her little face. She was speechless. She ran back over to him and flung her arms around his neck. 'Is it true? Is he really our dog, Mum?' she just kept asking me over and over again.

James was a little more cautious at first, having always been timid around dogs, so he ran in the opposite direction when he first saw Jasper. It didn't take him too long to realise that he had nothing to be worried about, as even at five months old Jasper was very calm and gentle, not as you'd imagine a five-month-old puppy to be at all. They very quickly became good friends.

So, at last, their dream of having a dog had finally come true for them. It had taken some doing, but been worth it just to see their little faces. There were a fair few tears of joy that day, certainly from me and my dad, and do you know what? I do believe I even saw a little tear in Gary's eye.

'Yes, that's another good idea of mine. I told you we needed to get a dog!' he said, with a wink and a smile.

So that's how Jasper ended up with the Mitchells. Meant to be, I think. But be careful what you wish for because, believe it or not, we did manage to get a dog that actually doesn't know how to bark! Now, had we needed a guard dog, we might have been a little disappointed. Lucky we didn't, because, to this day, we've never actually heard him bark!

He does shit from time to time! ... But he never, ever barks!

One other furry friend who took up residence at the Mitchells and deserves a little mention is Penelope the hamster. Abbie was sixteen when she took it upon herself to buy her own pet and keep it in her bedroom. This meant, in her world – that being the world of a hormonal teenager – if she bought it with her own money and kept it in her bedroom then Gary didn't have a say in the matter. To be fair, he might never have known Penelope the hamster was even living in our house had Abbie not decided to bring her downstairs with her to watch the telly one evening when Gary was at work. One minute, Penelope was sitting calmly, all snuggled up on Abbie's knee. Then when Abbie looked down again, Penelope had decided to go walkabout. A frenzied search followed as we desperately tried to find her before Gary returned home. We didn't.

The three of us were extremely confused as we could here intermittent scratching noises but couldn't see her anywhere. The moment we realised she had managed to burrow her way into the lining of the leather sofa, we knew we were all in big trouble as I'm sure you can imagine how pleased Gary was as he cut a hole in the side of the new sofa in order to rescue her. His silence as he worked said it all. She amazingly survived that little adventure, and despite that, and eating a small patch of Abbie's brand new carpet in her bedroom, she was a lovely little pet. Then, two years later, she, too, took her final resting place in our garden.

Words of Wisdom

Don't give up. Stick to your guns. It's inevitable you'll crack them in time. Plant the seed, then leave them with it, and wait until they actually believe it was their idea in the first place. It works every time, with every man.

Now, I'm all for mixing pets with children – I think it's a good thing – but do make sure you're prepared for feeding, cleaning and walking duties. As much as they'll promise to take their turn, please know when the initial excitement has worn off it's all going to be left to you.

27

Please keep your seats if you are riding again

After a fantastic holiday in Australia visiting my sister, we'd decided to stop off, on our way home, in Dubai. Such a busy, fast place, it was quite a shock to the system after our three weeks in Australia, where everyone had been so laid back and chilled. Eventually we emerged from the very hectic airport. First the heat hit you – as the temperature was around 45 degrees it felt like we were walking into a furnace. The noise levels were as high as the skyscrapers. Roads, which all seemed to be five lanes wide and crammed full with cars, were all hooting their horns impatiently.

Our hotel, when we finally found it, was nice, and the air conditioning was very welcome to us all, with a large swimming pool on the rooftop, which we couldn't wait to get into. As exciting as it was having a rooftop pool, it did feel rather like you were jumping into a very warm bath, thus doing little to actually cool us down. The temperature was unbelievably hot; we'd never experienced anything like this before. You'd think that having spent the last three weeks in Australia we'd have been somewhere near to being acclimatised. There was no doubt about it: air conditioning was your only saving grace. We learnt very quickly to stay inside throughout the daytime and only venture out after the sun had gone down, when it was ever so slightly cooler.

Abbie was now thirteen and James was five. It was a good way to break up the journey home, and Gary's cousin, Janet, lived there. She was very kind, offering to show us all the sights – which was just as well, because left to our own devices I don't think we'd have ever come out of our hotel.

There were no more 'G'day mate's from the locals as we walked by. Everyone seemed to be moving extremely fast to get to wherever it was they were going. It would appear they had no time at all for us.

We did try to walk along the beach once, but the sand was so hot on your feet a walk soon became a sprint – something I wouldn't recommend in those temperatures. We saved our exploring until the evenings, which were spent with Janet when she'd finished work. She tried to fit in as much sightseeing as she could for us, and this was great as she'd lived there for about five years and new the places to visit.

The four days seemed to pass quickly, and before we knew it our last day had arrived.

Janet said, 'Oh I must take you to see my favourite building. It has ninety floors, you'll love it. The elevator is on the outside of the building and it's all glass. The views are amazing.'

She wasn't wrong – it was probably the biggest building we'd ever seen. Looking up at it from the ground as we approached, you could hardly see the top. As we were arriving there just after seven, it was all lit up for the evening. There were a lot of people about, and the restaurant on the bottom floor was packed.

Security very high, as it was in most places. The security guard was asking us plenty of questions as to who we were and why we were there.

'We just wanted to have a little look and maybe take the kids up in the lift to the ninetieth floor,' Janet told him. It really was one of those fantastic buildings you see on the television.

'Wow! Look, Dad! That tower goes right up into the sky.'

James was blown away. It was huge. Apparently, there was a bar on the top floor, but unfortunately the porter who was in charge of the lift that evening couldn't allow the children to go up there. They did have a very strict drinking policy in the country – it wasn't easy for us to get a drink so I could understand why the kids weren't going to be allowed anywhere near a bar. They were both gutted, though, as we'd been talking about going in the glass lift all day.

'Oh can't we just go up Mum? Please, please, please?' Abbie begged.

As we were trying to explain to the kids why we weren't allowed up, I noticed Janet chatting and smiling with the porter.

'Right, he said we can take Abbie up, as she looks old enough, but we can only go to the top floor and not into the bar. James, I'm afraid, is definitely too young, so we can't allow him up. He'll have to stay here.'

So the three of them excitedly ran to press the button for the lift to come down.

Gary looked back at James. 'Ah, sorry, mate. We'll get you a big ice cream when we come back down.'

They all jumped excitedly into the lift and in a flash they were gone. James looked at me, a little tear welling up in his eye. He'd not been in bed before eleven for the last four nights and was shattered.

'Oh I'm so sorry, James. You're just too young, darling,' I told him, giving him a cuddle.

To be honest, I was quite relieved. I welcomed any excuse to stay on the ground floor, which was exactly where I'd fully intended to stay and just wave to them all. So off they went, zooming up at great speed; it went so fast, it was more like a ride at the fairground than a lift. I looked at James as a tear trickled down his little cheek; my heart sank for him. The porter had also clocked James's sadness and was obviously feeling guilty.

'Look, you two, you can take him up, but just on to the eightieth floor, or I'll be in big trouble.'

'Yah! Come, on Mummy!' cheered James, grabbing my hand and dragging me towards the lift doors.

Oh no. What does he mean, just me and James? My heart started to pound in my head and I suddenly felt quite faint. I really don't like lifts and heights – or speed, for that matter.

'No, no, it's fine, really. Thank you anyway. I don't want you getting into trouble on our account. We can just wait for them,' I said, hoping he would change his mind.

'Mummy, Mummy, please can we go? Please?!' James was jumping up and down and swinging on my arm.

How could I let him down now and not take him up? After all the palaver, we finally now had permission. Oh dear, it was all down to me. I couldn't possibly let him down now, could I? If only the porter had just let him go up with Gary. I never had any intention of going up in the first place.

'Come on, then.' Putting on a brave face, I grabbed his hand. 'Let's go do this.'

I picked James up so he could press the button up to the eightieth floor, and in seconds the lift arrived, not giving me any time to think about what I was doing. No sooner had we got in than the door shut and we were off. It really was like a fairground ride. I quickly grabbed his hand; he was looking out of the glass sides whilst I was facing the wall.

'Look how high we're going, Mummy! Wee! It's like being in a rocket!'

Very tentatively, I turned round to look for a second. Then I quickly turned back to face the wall.

'Oh yes, it's fantastic, James,' I managed to squeak.

Glancing at the numbers changing as we flew past each floor, in my state of panic I seemed to have forgotten there were ninety floors to this building, as all I remembered was the porter saying we were going to the eightieth floor. Someone must have already called the lift up to the ninetieth floor before we got in, which was probably the reason why it had set off almost instantly as the doors had closed. I was kind of thinking the eightieth floor was the last floor, so you can imagine my panic and horror when we got up to the eightieth floor and it didn't stop. Instead, we just kept going at great speed. Hysteria set in instantly.

As scenes from *Charlie and the Chocolate Factory* flashed into my mind – you know, the bit where the elevator flies out of the top of the building – I grabbed James and threw us both on to the floor. To this day I have no idea why – it must have been instinct, because if we were going through the top of the building surely we'd be safer on the deck! Wouldn't we? I wasn't even looking at the numbers anymore; my eyes were tightly closed and my hands were over James's head, pinning him down to the floor with me. Then, suddenly, it felt like we'd come to a standstill. There was silence, and I dared to open one eye only to find there was a group of people staring down at us as we had now arrived on the top floor and the lift doors had opened. Understandably, they were all looking down at James and me huddled in a ball on the floor. I have no idea what they must have been thinking, and as I don't speak Arabic there was no way of explaining to them why James and I were in the crash position on the floor of the lift.

Clambering to our feet and dusting ourselves off, we walked past them while keeping our heads down, and as quickly as we could walked out of the lift. James had gone very quiet; he wasn't quite sure what had just happened. Nevertheless, we were now here on the ninetieth floor, the one we weren't supposed to be on. I knew we had to get off this floor and back down quite sharpish, before our friendly porter lost his job. At this point I was considering taking the stairs, but I had to be real – we were ninety floors up and, even in my greatest fear, I knew there was no way I could walk down them all, never mind James. We had to get back into that lift – either that or be air-lifted down. So I reluctantly picked James up so he could press the button once more to call the lift back for us. I felt very nervous. The last thing I wanted to do was get back in there, but whilst we were waiting for it to arrive, I started to ponder on what had just happened. It was only then I began to realise it was just a calculation error on my part and that in my panic I'd miscounted and misjudged the floors. So as a little tear tried to escape from my eye, a nervous smile was also creeping across my face. How could I be so stupid? As if we were going to fly out of the building. In a lift.

'Okay, James, are you ready to go back down?' I said with an awkward smile.

I pretended what had just happened was all completely normal. He didn't seem quite as excited as he'd done on the way up, but then who could blame him? The lift arrived, we got back in and James pressed the button for the ground floor and once again we set off at top speed. Now, in my attempt to act normal and redeem James's confidence, I did manage to turn around this time and look out of the glass elevator at the amazing night view over Dubai. Indeed, it was pretty special.

'Look over there, Mummy. I think that tower is bigger than this one!' James shouted very excitedly and seemingly back to his usual self again.

As I'd spent the journey going up with my eyes closed and facing the wall, far too scared to look out, there were a few things I'd failed to notice. One of these things was that there was actually a restaurant halfway up the tower, around floor thirty, I believe. I now know that the lift actually goes right through the middle of this restaurant. I think you might know what's coming.

As we approached the thirtieth floor I could see this restaurant coming closer and closer as we zoomed down towards it. Unfortunately for poor James, the terror wasn't quite over yet, as in my mind I thought we must have been approaching the ground floor, where

I'd seen a restaurant when we arrived earlier. I could see it getting nearer and nearer, and we didn't appear to be slowing down at all – I'm afraid panic had once again taken over me. It seemed to me to be plummeting through the middle of a restaurant.

This is exactly what it was doing, and had I had my eyes open on the way up I would have known that this lift travelled right through the centre of the restaurant on floor thirty. I kind of hope now, looking back, that even though we were travelling at a fantastic speed, someone in that restaurant did glance up from their meal, just for a second, to see what must have been a hilarious sight. Once again, I thought it had failed to stop and we were going through the ground floor. My mothering instinct kicked in, only this time I grabbed James, pulling him towards the wall with me, pinning us both to the side of the elevator with all my strength. Terrified, and bracing myself for the inevitable 'thud' that was about to happen. I looked across at James for what I believe to be the last time: he was now staring at me as if to say, 'How did I end up with you as my mum?'

Bracing myself and him ready to hit the ground at speed – as for the second time in only five minutes I truly believed we were both about to die – I actually now felt numb. I think my body had worn itself out with fight or flight. I couldn't see the expression on the faces of the people inside the restaurant but I feel sure they were as confused as we were.

Then I felt a slight change in the speed of the lift. I dared to open my eyes once more, this time to find that we were actually only just approaching the ground floor. I couldn't believe it! I'd done it again – completely freaked out for no reason and put poor James through yet another nightmare. His little face was now ashen. I don't think he had any idea what had just happened, but I'm sure he sensed, by the fear running through me, that it must have been something big. As the doors finally opened at the end of our hell ride, Gary, Abbie and Janet were waiting with great big smiles on their faces.

'It was fantastic, wasn't it? So glad they eventually let you two go up as well!' shouted Gary, full of enthusiasm. They'd obviously had the best time.

'Yes,' said James, not quite as enthusiastically.

Strangely, neither James or I mentioned what had just happened;

I think we were both in shock. We sat quietly in the car on the way back to the hotel, listening to those three chatting away merrily about their terrific experience.

It wasn't until the next morning when we drove past the building on our way back to the airport that I suddenly started to laugh – a chuckle at first, but soon becoming uncontrollable. In fact, I was laughing so much that tears were streaming down my face, and I could hardly speak to explain to Gary what I was finding so funny. He started laughing too, though he didn't quite know yet what at. Once I managed to get the tale out, though, neither he nor Abbie could believe that all that had gone on and that neither James nor I had mentioned anything about it. James, who I think was perhaps still a little traumatised by the whole experience, didn't join in the laughter at first, but after listening to the rest of the family for some time, he did, in the end, start to smile – just a little.

'I can't believe you haven't told us this till now,' Gary and Abbie both said.

'Well, I suppose it didn't seem all that funny last night. I think we were both still in shock.'

It kept us all amused as we fought our way back through the busy airport, possibly helping to keep my mind off getting on a plane. On the plus side, at least I wasn't going home in an elevator!

Words of Wisdom

So was James scarred from the experience I'd so wrongly put him through? I think, for a time, yes he definitely was, as the terror in his eyes when confronted with a lift said it all.

I'm very pleased to say that now, nine years on, he can get into a lift without even thinking about it, and that's without any counselling. Nevertheless, for some strange reason he refuses to take the lift with me. I've tried on several occasions to walk in after him, only to be met by his glare. Not surprisingly, I do prefer to take the stairs when it's feasible, but if need be I'll hang back and wait for the next lift to come along.

28

Against all odds

When you have a fourteen-year-old daughter to keep entertained, your choice of holiday is quite important as they don't need any encouragement to be stroppy, moody or, indeed, to kick off. Unfortunately, in this particular year the funds weren't running very high and we had no choice of holiday destination: it was camping in Northumberland or staying at home. I did seriously contemplate staying at home but felt that any break had to be better than nothing.

The journey in exceptionally strong gale-force winds and driving rain wasn't at all uplifting, not for any of us, and as Abbie sat staring out of the window with earphones firmly planted in her ears, I felt sure that she was daydreaming that soon it would all be over. James was sat with Jasper on his knee, unable to move, but as we'd brought almost everything we owned from home, just in case, there really wasn't any room left in the boot for a dog. Eventually we arrived at our campsite, which wasn't perhaps looking its best, with the backdrop of low cloud and fog.

Nevertheless Gary, our ever-optimistic tour guide, told us, 'It just looks like this because it's raining. It'll look different again in the morning, in the sunshine. You'll see.'

Abbie and I went to inspect the toilets. It was official: we were staying at a dump. We had no choice and would have to use the toilets, but neither of us girls had any intention of having a shower in there. After unpacking, we all put on our waterproofs and set off to explore. Not far from our site we came across a golf club; children were allowed in, and the evening menu looked nice. This was promising.

Waking up the next morning to the sound of the rain on the caravan was a little disheartening, but Jasper needed walking so we went to find the beach. We found a beautiful one about thirty minutes away from where we were staying, spreading over miles and almost empty – maybe not too surprisingly on a day like this. Well, naturally, Jasper had a great time; he wasn't bothered about the weather at all and just ran and ran up and down on the sands. Abbie chose not to leave the car this particular morning and instead sat looking out of the window with her earphones still in. She'd removed them a couple of times since we'd arrived, though only to get washed and go to sleep. Returning to the car with a rather wet and sandy Jasper, we then drove round to see if there were any indoor activities to be found.

'I just want to go shopping, and can I have my ears pierced again?' Abbie asked for the twentieth time since we'd left home. I looked over at Gary.

'We'll see,' he said.

There was a sigh from the back seat. I looked round at her and gave her a promising wink. It was a start; at least he hadn't said no this time. That evening, after settling a very tired dog down, we walked to the golf club for some tea. There was a little play area outside and it had just about stopped raining, so James was very happy. The food was great and after a large glass of coke Abbie took her earphones out and did begin to talk to us, perhaps for the first time since we'd arrived. We all walked back to the caravan feeling much happier. I'm sure the bottle of wine might've had something to do with this, and the fact that it had now finally stopped raining was, I think, making us all feel a little more cheery. Maybe tomorrow was going to be a better day.

It wasn't! The rain seemed relentless, although we did battle through it and on to the beach once more, with a very happy dog. James had been dying to get into the sea since we'd arrived, but with the wind and rain the sea looked rather uninviting, so we tried to put him off for as long as we possibly could, which turned out to be until now. Following another day of his constant nagging, Gary finally gave in. Fortunately, we'd brought a wetsuit for him – a lesson learnt many years ago after countless holidays in the rain. It was true: the 'Mitchell Cloud' did seem to find us wherever we travelled – something that amongst our family and friends we were now well renowned for. Gary helped an already shivering James into the wetsuit and he happily ran off towards the sea. So we now had a happy dog, a happy seven-year-old and a suicidal fourteen-year-old. Two out of three ain't bad!

It was back to the golf club that night. James went out to play once more on the drenched play area, Gary and I drank wine, and Abbie – again, after a glass of coke – decided she would take her earphones out and chat with us.

Anticipating her dad was a little tipsy, she felt now was a good time to ask once more about having her ears pierced. She'd been wanting her ears re-piercing for some time. Gary, understandably, had been reluctant to let her – this was after all the palaver we'd gone through the last time they were done (refer to chapter 33!). To be fair, though, the way the week was going we really did need some kind of incentive for poor Abbie to try keep her spirits up. Gary promised to think about it. Don't you just hate it when your dad says he'll think about it? You know this means you have to be on your best behaviour until he's decided to stop thinking about it. With this in mind, though, the next couple of days were a little jollier as Abbie's mood did seem to lift, a little.

The trips to the beach, regardless of the weather, continued for the next couple of days. We did manage to finally get Abbie out of the car and on to the beach, as the rain had at last subsided. She enjoyed watching Jasper racing up and down the sand, and I do think we saw a little smile more than once that morning. It was actually good fun walking with the wind behind you, pushing you along, and we didn't quite realise just how far we'd walked – until it was time to turn round and walk back towards the car. Timed perfectly with the return of the rain, this task, with the now gale-force wind blowing against us and driving the rain into our faces, was a real battle. Walking forwards was almost impossible.

Luckily, with the noise of the sea and the wind we couldn't quite hear what was coming out of Abbie's mouth, but I'm guessing by the look on her face it wasn't very pleasant. We all just seemed to put our heads down and make our own way back to where we thought the car was. Jasper was still very happy sniffing and running around, seemingly un-perturbed by the weather. Looking forward was virtually impossible as the wind took your breath and the rain stung your face – as did the sand that was being scooped up and blown around the beach. Was this really August?

Abbie was first back to the car, closely followed by Gary and then James. I came in last place as I was waiting for Jasper, who really was the only one still having a great time out there. After finally getting Jasper and all the sand that was now stuck to him into the car, I opened the front door to find three dripping wet people with very wind-beaten faces looking back at me. I was by now absolutely soaked – so glad I'd taken the time to put mascara on this morning. At last, after a final fight against the wind, I threw myself into the car before the door slammed shut behind me. Quite breathless by now, I looked behind me into the back seat. A small grin appeared on Abbie's face; I could tell she was trying to hold it back because she was so angry, but she couldn't help herself and she started to chuckle, then James and Gary joined in. I glanced in the mirror: my hair was stuck flat to my very wet and red face and I had two thick black lines of mascara rolling down my cheeks. Shaking my head, I too started laughing, saying, 'I really wanted to go to Spain this year!'

After sitting there and all laughing uncontrollably for the next five minutes or so, Gary finally announced, 'Come on, we'd better get going. The car's steamed up with all these wet bodies in here.'

Back at the campsite I broke my promise to myself of not showering for a week as I was so cold. Actually, it wasn't that bad in there. Despite it being summer, the site owners had decided to put the heating on. Abbie took the plunge too, also being pleasantly surprised. The water was very warm and there was plenty of it.

That night at the golf club, James once more enjoyed playing out on the damp playground, whilst Abbie and I managed to convince Gary, with the help of a couple of beers, that it was a great idea to let her have her ears pierced again. So the next morning, before Gary had a chance to change his mind, we were up and out the door, on our way to the jewellers. Abbie never stopped talking all the way there, which was a refreshing change. It all went well and she was thrilled with her new earrings. At last Abbie was happy, very happy indeed. James, at this point, I'm afraid, was bored; he really didn't do shopping of any form.

The rain continued to fall.

'Come on, let's go back and watch a film. That'll cheer us all up'. We'd brought along with us, amongst other things, the DVD player, and one of Gary's mates from work had lent him some nice family films.

'Yes, I'll make us all a nice hot chocolate, and you lot can choose a film,' I added.

After a good half hour's discussion – well, argument – we eventually managed to all agree on a film. It started so well: it was great for all the family with a bit of adventure, romance and a nice storyline. A great choice. We were all enjoying it and settling in with our hot chocolates when suddenly, right out of the blue, none of us saw it coming, one of the main characters, a child, just died. It was horrendous – we were all absolutely heartbroken. I've never been good with sad films, so it's not surprising I was crying. But the rest of them, they're usually fine; they normally just sit laughing at me getting upset. Not with this one, though. This was so very sad even Gary couldn't hold the tears back. By the time it had finished, I was exhausted from crying uncontrollably. For a second time I had mascara smudged right across my face only this time no one found it funny as they were all too devastated.

We all just sat there staring at the blank screen when it finished. Gary eventually broke the silence with a wobbly voice, saying, 'Well, I'm going to have to have a word with Mark when I go back into work next week. He told me that we'd all love that film!'

On the plus side, it was now just about time to get ready to go out to the golf club for our tea. We started to get ready in silence, all lost in our own thoughts. Over tea it was decided this night was to be our last in Northumberland; the weather wasn't looking to improve and I think we'd all done very well under the circumstances not to kill each other, so now was possibly a good time go home, before we did. It had certainly had its ups and its downs, but this is probably one of the holidays that sticks in all our minds.

Reflecting on it now, it still brings a smile to my face. What an earth were we thinking?

Words of Wisdom

Maybe the moral behind this story would be not to give up before you've started. The holiday that seemed at first to be heading for disaster did actually turn out to be quite good. Character-building, I think Gary called it. Jasper certainly had the best time, and he did make that holiday. James was content for most of the time, and even Abbie – in the midst of the teenaged years – managed a few laughs here and there. Returning home with her ears pierced made her extremely happy. Had we stayed there till the end of the week and not come home early, then the outcome could have been quite different. My only advice here: don't push it, quit whilst you're ahead.

29

They think it's all over,
is it now?

I'd never really looked forward to the day that James would want to join a football team. I knew it would happen at some point, but I was kind of dreading it. A few of my friends who had older boys had already warned me and told me the nightmare tales of endless muddy kits to wash and football boots to clean – not to mention the early Sunday mornings stood around a freezing cold football pitch.

'Oh, I won't be doing any of that, it's men's business. Gary can take him. I hate football, and as for muddy football boots, he can clean them himself,' I vowed.

Those were my thoughts on football. I'd done the gymnastics with Abbie and thoroughly enjoyed it, but football? No way. So when James asked to play, Gary took him down to our local team to see how he went on.

'He loved it. He wasn't very good, but he loved it' was the outcome of his first training session.

'Well, it's early days. As long as he's enjoyed it that's all that matters,' I added.

The following week I went down with them, only for a nosey to see what went on. I got chatting to a couple of the other mums and before I knew it I found myself returning there, of my own free will, with James every Saturday morning. It meant that I could take the dog with me and throw his ball for him whilst James was training, killing two birds with one stone. This soon became our Saturday morning routine. I still didn't really understand the game; however, James did seem to do a lot of running up and down the pitch. He was never anywhere near the ball, but he seemed more than happy with his little self.

When the first match was mentioned it was all very exciting. James got picked for the team – I believe he was to play in defence, and this was great news for him as one of his best friends from school, Sam, was in goal.

Sunday morning arrived and I felt quite nervous for them all. Gary was working days, unfortunately, so couldn't be there. I was quite emotional when they all came out on to the pitch in the team kits – they were all so small and cute. The whistle blew and they were off; it was a bit of a free for all, and it felt like we were watching a running race rather than a football match, as all eighteen players were racing up and down the pitch after the ball at the same time.

'Remember your positions, boys!' the team coach shouted at them all.

I'm guessing that with all the excitement of playing in a real match they'd all forgotten what positions they were meant to be in and just what it was they were supposed to be doing. After half-time and a good team talk, they'd all been reminded once more to stay in their own positions and not to just run after the ball. The second half began with a slightly more organised team and as the game went on the ball did seem to be in the opponent's box much more than it was in ours. I believe this was great for our team because it meant that we were the more dominant of the two sides. Unfortunately, though, it did mean that a certain James was beginning to lose interest and become a little bit bored. I could see a vacant look on his face, which was worrying because James is either switched on or switched off – there really is no in-between for him. I took my attention away from him to watch the rest of the game for a few minutes, and when I looked back I couldn't see him at all.

Scanning the pitch I located him sat on the ground with his best friend, Sam, the goalie. They were both just on the edge of the circle.

'What an earth are they doing?' I asked Sam's mum.

They looked like they were having a discussion about something. Now, I don't pretend to know anything much about football, but even I know it's not good if your goalie and your defender are sat down having a little chat in the middle of a game.

'What are they doing? Are they picking the mud out of their boots?' Sam's mum asked me.

'Yes, I think they are' was my surprised reply.

Thats exactly what they were doing. It was their debut match and both goalie and defender were sat cross-legged on the floor picking all the mud from in-between the studs of their new football boots. Thank goodness Gary was working and not here to see this. Sam's dad was there, though, and I can't repeat what was coming out of his mouth.

'James, Sam, what are you doing?' Jess and I shouted at them both, as I'd noticed the ball had finally made it out of the opposition's box and was heading their way.

'Quick, get up, boys! The ball's coming!'

Alas, too late was the cry: the ball came flying past them both, directly over their heads and into the net. Not overly difficult when there's no goalie present. Perhaps not the best start to a football career, then.

Despite the bad start and after a few firm words from the coach they were forgiven by him and the rest of the team mates. They both went on to play for the team for a good few years and regardless of my promise not to get involved I carried on supporting them every weekend, come rain or shine – wouldn't have missed it for the world. It was great to see them all coming on, and every now and then they actually won a game. I'd often return to the car extremely pale with a blue tinge to my lips, needing to soak in the bath for quite some time in order to get myself back to a healthier looking colour. It can't have been all that bad because I kept going back for more, week after week. I can't say I was too upset when the odd game was cancelled here and there due to a frozen or waterlogged pitch.

Apart from the entertainment on the pitch it was always good to see parents behaving badly. On several occasions I've watched in amazement whilst dads and mums have run on to the pitch to have a word with the referee. I've listened to shouting, often swearing, and I've seen a great deal of tantrums – and that's mainly the mums. It was worthwhile turning up just for that some weeks and it did stop me thinking about how cold I was, if only for a few minutes. The other thing I'd vowed when James started to play regularly, and when I found myself turning up every week to matches, was that I would only go to support them whilst they were little and cute.

'I'm going to stop coming when their hormones kick in. I don't want to be here when they start swearing and spitting!'

James is coming up to fifteen now, and surprisingly I'm still going to watch each Sunday. I have witnessed both kids and teens play, and feel sure – due to the size that they've all now become – that the hormones have well and truly kicked in.

As for washing his own football boots, I've purposely on many an occasion left them outside for him to wash only to find them still there a week later, the day before a match. It would then come down to who it bothers the most. As he didn't care what colour his boots were, inevitably I would be the one who ended up cleaning them for him, mainly because I was worried about what the other parents would think. It's safe to say, then, that I've been cleaning his football boots for around about nine years!

Words of Wisdom

Can you learn anything from me about football? Well, I still don't understand the offside rule. But does anybody?

I'm not even that good at getting boots clean, despite my nine years of practice. I think what I've learnt here is to never underestimate the power of being a mum – you may find yourself doing things that you though you never would just to watch your children enjoy and achieve their goals.

30

Confused? you will be

Non-uniform days at school have always been greatly looked forward to in our house. It's a refreshing change for the kids to be able to wear their own clothes. Even more exciting is when they can wear fancy dress costumes for school, something they've done plenty of times when it's been Book Week and other events. We always got into the full swing of dressing up and went all out to look the part.

James was about eight when this little tale took place. Having come home from school on the Tuesday evening, my friend Alice and her daughter, Neve, had come over to visit, something they often did on their way home from school. Alice and I had known each other since we were eight, and Neve and Lewis were the same age, so the kids would play together whilst we had a chat over a coffee or two.

It was the Thursday morning before I noticed James had brought a letter home from school the previous Tuesday evening which I hadn't seen. Eventually I came across it on a little pile of paperwork that constantly lives on the kitchen worktop – the one that never really gets any less because you just keep adding to it. The letter said that on Friday they were having a soccer day at school to raise some money for the sports department. There would also be a Bradford City football player coming into school to organise a penalty shoot-out. The kids could go to school that day in their football kits. Should they support a specific team then they were allowed to wear that kit, as long as they donated a pound.

'This sounds great, James. You can wear your Liverpool kit that Granddad bought you.'

'Yes, I will,' he replied as he was watching the telly.

Friday came. I had no problem getting James up and ready for school as he was very excited about putting his football kit on. As we walked up to school, he looked very proud in his Liverpool colours.

'I'm going to score loads of goals, Mummy, when we do the penalty shoot-out,' James said as he skipped round the corner and through the school gates.

All the mums were smiling and saying how nice he looked. We headed straight for the office so that he could pay his pound for the privilege of not wearing his uniform. The head teacher smiled at James as he walked in, looking him up and down.

'Morning. Here's James's money for the football day.'

'Sorry, what's that?' she replied, sounding very confused.

'The football day?' I repeated a bit louder. At this point my heart did start to sink a little, as I noticed a couple more of the teachers had come out of the staff room to see what was going on.

'I'm sorry, Mrs Mitchell . . . Not sure what you're talking about.'

'The letter we had on Tuesday saying Bradford City were coming in for a penalty shoot-out with the kids?'

She looked at me completely blank. 'Really not sure what you're talking about. I'm sorry.'

I looked down at James, who by now was the same colour as his Liverpool kit; I think I was much the same. His little hand had suddenly gone all sweaty, and it slipped out of mine.

'Oh dear. Okay, it looks like I've got something wrong here. Shall I take James home and get him changed, then?' I was completely shocked. Had I dreamt the whole thing up? Maybe I had. Poor James.

'It's up to you, James. You can stay dressed in your kit if you want to,' the headmistress very kindly said to him.

'Yes, okay, then I will,' he replied very calmly.

So that's what he did, No questions asked, he skipped into school quite proud to be in his Liverpool kit. Had that happened with Abbie I feel it would have been a very different story. She would have been mortified and probably would never have spoken to me again. The teachers disappeared into their classrooms and I went back home, completely confused. What had happened there? I'd seen the letter and read it; surely if I'd got the date wrong they'd have at least known something about it at school. Well, it was a mystery to me. Re-reading the letter when I got home only added to my confusion.

Whilst in the park that afternoon with the dog, Alice rang me. As we were chatting, she mentioned that Neve hadn't been very happy going to school that morning.

'Oh. Why? What . . . what's wrong with her?' I asked.

'Well it was this stupid "soccer day". All her friends were excited about the Bradford City football team coming, but she hates football and wasn't looking forward to—'

'The what?' I had to stop her mid-sentence. 'Sorry, who's coming today? Did you say Bradford City?'

'Yes, they'll be there all day doing penalty shoot-outs with the kids. I think that's really good of them, don't you?'

'Oh no, you're never going to believe what I've done, Alice.'

Then followed quite a long pause from her, as she waited for me to stop laughing so I could eventually tell her what I'd done. Meanwhile, whilst I was trying to contain my laughter, Alice was giggling away, safe in the knowledge that this story was going to be worth waiting for. When I finally managed to get the tale out, we pieced things together in-between fits of laughter: Neve must have put the letter down on the worktop on Tuesday when she called only for me to find it two days later. Being the lazy reader I've always been, I failed to miss the top right-hand side of the paper that clearly said the name of Neve's school on it and not the name of James's! We laughed for quite some time as Alice visualised poor James being the only one at his school in his football kit. She thought it was even more funny that he was happy to stay wearing it. That's James – he really has no interest in clothes. In fact, if I didn't put his clothes out ready for him in a morning then I'm sure he would just go to school naked. Tears were streaming down our faces by that point.

Well, at least the mystery was solved and I now knew I wasn't losing the plot. I couldn't wait to get to school and have a word with the teachers with an explanation – which was met with laughter from them – and when word got round to the parents, I'm sure they also had a good chuckle at my expense too.

Words of Wisdom

I'm still able to make everyone laugh at school, then – the only difference being that I'm actually not trying anymore. I think this is what they mean when they say the joke's on you. It's payback time for all those teachers whose classes I disrupted many years ago – a good lesson to learn for any children reading this, who enjoy being the class clown, as I did. If I'd listened more and paid attention whilst at school, perhaps my reading skills might have been up to par and this, alongside many other errors, could have been avoided.

31

Reports so far

Being far from a scholar during my school years, I didn't feel in a position to lecture my two when it came to exams and report time. My only advice to them was if they didn't at least give it a try, then they'd only regret it in later years, as I have done. Most of my school reports hadn't quite made the journey home. I realised from quite a young age that it would be much safer for me if my parents didn't ever see them. The few they did get to see, the ones which I classed as my best ones, they weren't too thrilled with. It's isn't surprising, though, when they included comments like 'I'm thinking of having an armchair brought into the workshop, so that Joanne doesn't have to strain herself too much whilst in my class!'

As you can imagine, my parents weren't overly impressed with that, and I suppose, as a parent myself now, I can see why.

Keeping this in mind I've never put a great deal of pressure on my two. I've always felt it was far more important that they were happy and had good friends.

Abbie's reports were always pretty good. She had to work hard to get good results, but she was prepared to do that. So our school report evenings for her were usually very happy times. Despite this, in the midst of those teenage years, her reports didn't seem to reflect her at all. In fact, they often sounded like they could have belonged to someone else, describing her as a polite, well mannered, patient young lady, which didn't tally up at all with this stroppy, impatient madam that now seemed to be living at home with us. She came across as a true little angel according to all her teachers.

'That's a lovely report, Abbie, but can you give us yours please, and give whoever's report this is back to them!' would be Gary's sarcastic remark after reading it.

The general consensus between Gary and I was that we must be doing something right if she's well behaved at school.

James? Slightly different. He wasn't a bad lad at school, by any means but he did seem to struggle with his concentration, often being in trouble for staring out of the window during class instead of listening to the teacher. All the school reports in primary school were much the same, for instance, 'If James could keep his concentration, I'm sure he could be brilliant.'

This was so true. If James decided he was going to do something and he was interested enough, he would always give it his all. For example, when the circus entertainer came to school to show them how to use the diabolo, he was mesmerised, almost obsessed! He bought one that evening online and couldn't wait for it to arrive. It was then straight on to YouTube, sitting for hours and hours, watching a bit, then practising. This went on for weeks. By the end of the month he could do all the tricks the man had shown him at school.

A week or so later a few of his friends were becoming interested in the diabolo; they too purchased one, and before we knew it our whole street was filled with boys and girls of all ages playing with diabolos. The parents were happy and agreed that it was definitely much better for them than constantly being inside on their PlayStations.

He did exactly the same with the Rubik's Cube: he was determined to master it and I think he sat for two whole days over the weekend until, finally, he'd cracked that too. We just needed to find something at school that he found interesting, very interesting. His year three teacher summed him up pretty well when she wrote in his report, 'James always knows the answer to the question, if only he could remember the question!'

His favourite pastime that he excelled at in primary school was staring out of the window. This, alongside his ability to move no faster than a snail, didn't seem to be improving at all. He was always late for school, despite my efforts to have him ready to leave on time each morning.

There would always be something important he had to do, which would result in him usually dashing back up the stairs to his bedroom just as we were about to leave the house. On our way to school we often had to return for something he'd forgotten. As you can imagine I spent plenty of my time worrying about how he'd cope in upper school. I envisaged he'd spend a great deal of his time in trouble for being late, forgetful and generally zoomed into another planet, and I feared he'd be coming home each evening with a planner filled with comments. However, surprisingly, he didn't – in fact, quite the opposite: he managed to get through that first year without collecting any adverse comments. The school report told a story of quite a different boy, one who still had the tendency to zone out from time to time but seemed quite eager to learn. My fears and worries, then, were all in vain.

Words of Wisdom

It took me a while to work this one out and I'm not saying it's easy by any means, but from where I'm standing, the best way for them to learn is to just push them out of the nest and then watch them learn to fly.

It's probably best I don't give my advice on exams and school reports as I do feel that far too much pressure is put on our children (and indeed the poor teachers). I'm a true believer that a smile can take you anywhere you want to go.

32

Old enough to stay alone?

This is not a chapter totally about my children, but I did want to slip it in somewhere.

At James's primary school they would hold a disco about four times a year. In the first three years of school they were all welcome to go, but as they were still quite young a parent was asked to stay with them. James always enjoyed the school disco as this gave him chance to ask one of the girls from his class to be his girlfriend! As there were only eight girls and twenty-three boys in his class, it didn't take him long to get through them all. In fact, by year four I think he'd 'been out' with them all, some of them more than once. Having now reached year four, he was finally old enough to stay at the disco on his own.

The night of the disco, I was working late. Gary had come off nights and was in charge of the evening. He'd dropped a very excited James off at school and returned home, happy to have the house to himself for a couple of hours as there was a game of rugby due to be shown on the TV that evening.

I'd rung to check that all was going okay, and I said to Gary, 'When you go to collect James, would you take Jasper with you? He could do with a little walk.'

'Yes, will do, love' was his quick reply. He was no doubt eager to get me off the phone, as the game had now started.

Returning home later, I was very relieved to find both Gary and James sat watching the rugby, as I'd been a little concerned that Gary might have fallen asleep and forgotten to collect James.

'Had a good time, James?' I asked as I came in the room.

No reply. They were both focused on the telly – something I'd grown used to by now. I took myself upstairs and had a nice soak in the bath. When I came back downstairs at about ten o'clock, they were still sat there.

I went into the kitchen and shouted, 'Has anyone fed Jasper yet?'

No reply, again!

Starting to get a little tired of being ignored, I then went into the front room where they were both sat, mesmerised, looking at the TV. Raising my voice ever so slightly, I repeated, 'Has anyone fed Jasper?'

'No. Sorry, love,' Gary eventually replied.

A little cross that Gary hadn't thought to feed the poor dog, I proceeded to fill his bowl with some dog biscuits, making as much noise as I could whilst doing it – the dry biscuits going into a metal bowl can be pretty loud when poured from a great height. I was trying to make as much noise as possible – one, so that the dog would hear it and come running for his tea and two, to get Gary's attention to make a point that I was doing it. It seemed both these aims were to no avail. Now, anyone who's ever spent any time around our dog would know he's a very quiet animal. To our knowledge, we still don't think he knows how to bark; he's certainly not a dog that makes a great big fuss of you when you return home. We never have to brace ourselves when coming through the door like most dog owners. If he manages to get up and walk towards you with a gentle wag of his tail, then you'd consider yourself quite lucky.

This in mind, it was quite normal for us to not know exactly where he was whilst in the house, as he was so quiet. But he does like his food, so when after a few minutes I noticed that he still hadn't appeared, I shouted from the kitchen, 'Gary, where's Jasper? Is he in there with you?'

There was a delay, but then I heard a clambering noise and Gary shouting, 'Shit, shit, I've left him tied up outside school!'

'You've what!?' I shouted as I came running into the room. Gary nearly choked on his beer.

'I took him to school, like you said, but totally forgot about him. He's tied up outside school.'

'You've left him there? It's past 10 o'clock! Oh, Gary!'

He went running out of the door, followed by plenty of abuse. I couldn't believe it – the disco had finished at 8.30 and it was now nearly 10.30. I thought I was going to be sick. Pacing up and down whilst we were waiting for him to come back, all sorts of things were shooting through my mind. Surely if anybody had seen him tied to the school fence they would have rang us – our telephone number was clearly written on his collar. But what if somebody had stolen him? I couldn't bear the thought. Gary hadn't even twigged when I asked if anybody had fed the dog.

Unbelievable!

James sat very quiet, perhaps feeling a little guilty that he too had walked straight past Jasper at the school gates. In fairness to him, he didn't actually know Gary had taken Jasper in the first place. Abbie, being as verbal as she was at this stage, didn't stop for breath telling me how useless her dad was and that he just couldn't be trusted with anything. She was in the prime of those teen years so I just left her to get on with it, but to be honest at this point I was entitled to agree with her. How could anyone walk past their own dog at the school gates? I know he's mostly black and it was dark and being Jasper he wouldn't have made a noise when Gary and James walked past him like you'd expect a dog to do. You'd have thought something would have sparked Gary's memory – if not then, at least when he got back home.

Then after what seemed like forever, the door opened and Jasper's little nose came through first (I don't think Gary dare come in before him).

'Ah, Jasper! Thank goodness. You poor thing. Did that naughty Daddy just leave you?'

Everyone was trying to cuddle him at the same time, and he wasn't overly sure what was going on, but actually, for once, he did look pretty excited to see us all. Apparently, he was just laid down by the gates, where Gary had left him, patiently waiting. Obviously, no one else had noticed him tethered. Gary blamed it on the rugby – that and the fact that he'd just come off nights!

Of course, he did try to pin the blame on the dog. 'Well, he should have barked at me, or something, when I walked past him.'

We all know Jasper doesn't do barking. In fact, as Gary was the one who specifically stated when we were getting a dog that he didn't want one that barked all the time, I'm afraid we were having none of that; we all knew exactly who was to blame.

Words of Wisdom

Is there something to be learnt from this? Multi-tasking and men: they just don't go together. Stick to giving them one job to do at a time. Had I left Gary with only the one job to do – picking up James – then all would have been fine. But no, I pushed it by bringing the dog into the equation. Should have known better, really. For that, then, I only have myself to blame.

33

Bumps and tumbles

With the best will in the world, you're not going to get all the way through motherhood without a good few accidents, injuries and falls. It can start when they're still very young, most likely even before they're walking. I remember at least one of mine managed to roll themselves off the bed and on to the floor before I was even aware they were mobile. The classic has got to be the stairs, and despite how careful we may think we're being with them and regardless of how thorough our stair training seems to have been, there will always be that one time. It only takes a second – maybe the stair gate has been left open or perhaps they have suddenly decided they no longer need to come down steps on their bottoms. Add to that excitement and a bit of speed and you have a recipe for disaster. While the calamity often happens right before your very eyes, unfortunately there's absolutely nothing that you can do about it except pick them up again when they've finally landed. I'll never forget that awful feeling it left in my stomach, as both of mine have managed to misjudge the stairs at least once.

Being a gymnast for eight years, Abbie has done extremely well not to break anything apart from her little toe. Although after practising her trampolining skills on grandma and granddad's bed whilst on a sleepover one night, a couple of stitches were needed as she misjudged the landing, boycotting the bed completely and managing to land on the radiator head first. At the age of two, when we lived above the hair salon, she did manage to trip up one morning, cracking the side of her head on one of the metal-based heat lamps. She was, as usual, travelling at high speed, hitting it with some force.

There was a fair bit of blood and some tears, and then followed a huge black eye, but no stitches were required. The timing couldn't have been better: just two days before my brother's wedding, leaving us a constant reminder on all the wedding photos.

Another consequence of living above a hair salon with an inquisitive little one would be all the interesting things that are about for touching. A cut-throat razor, for instance, would most definitely be a no-no for a four-year-old. Despite being told many a time never to go anywhere near them, never mind touch one, curiosity eventually got the better of Abbie and she couldn't resist just a little look. This was one morning on her way to school when she'd spotted it had been left out in the salon. Having examined the razor, she soon realised just why I'd told her so many times not to touch it. Knowing that she might be in a lot of trouble for picking it up in the first place, she thought it best not to mention that there was rather a lot of blood coming from her finger. Instead, she wrapped some tissue around her hand and promptly hid it in her pocket for the walk up to school. I did think that she was unusually quiet that morning and perhaps a little paler than normal, but it wasn't until we reached the school gates that she eventually broke her silence.

'I think my finger's bleeding, Mummy.'

'Oh my goodness, it is. What an earth have you done?'

'I don't know,' she said as she started to cry. A good ploy – always turn on the tears if you think you're going to be in trouble (always works for me, even now!). As you can imagine, it was rather nasty – well, they're not called cut-throat razors for nothing, are they? Once in school, and with the help of the first aider, we managed to slow the bleeding down considerably, eventually stopping it enough to get a bandage on. Unbelievably, again, no stitches were needed. In the end we got to the bottom of what had happened that morning, Abbie had learned a few valuable lessons here, whilst managing to frighten herself half to death in the process, and I therefore felt there was no need for me to be too angry with her.

Probably the worst thing that ever happened for Abbie – and it wasn't really an accident – was when she had her ears pierced. She was ten years old and we'd eventually caved in due to peer pressure (something I said I'd never do). I'd wanted her to wait a little longer as I felt she was just a bit too young and maybe she wouldn't look after them properly. According to Abbie, though, she was the only girl in her whole class, and possibly school, that hadn't had them done yet.

She went along one day with her grandma, as I didn't think that I would be able to watch. Grandma said she was very brave, never flinched apparently, and that she was thrilled to bits with them. As for not being old enough to look after them, she proved us all wrong here by religiously bathing them in the solution both morning and night for the full six weeks. It wasn't until exactly five weeks and three days after they'd been pierced, whilst taking her jumper off one evening, she accidentally caught one. It didn't come out but it did give it quite a yank, leaving her ear sore and a little red. She was worried that because of this it wasn't going to heal up properly, and promptly started to cry.

'Don't worry, Abbie. They'll probably be healed up by now anyway. I can just put you some extra solution on and I'm sure all will be fine, darling,' I told her before she got into bed.

The next morning came and I'm afraid it looked like Mummy was wrong. Her ear was now twice its original size and we could no longer see the earring. She came running into my room in floods of tears. After a trip down to the doctors, it was decided that – as she wouldn't let the doctor go anywhere near her ear, even to just have a look – it was probably best we took her to hospital.

'Told you so. Told you she was too young' was Gary's helpful input.

'You can't say that. She's been brilliant with the solution – she's done it every morning and night. It's just unfortunate that her jumper caught it, that's all.'

The hospital staff were great, but unfortunately Abbie was not, as when any doctor or nurse tried to come anywhere near her, even to just have a look, she instantly started screaming – and I mean screaming like she was being murdered. Now, I know it was sore, but after two hours of this I was beginning to tire. I don't think the staff were too happy about the situation either.

'Abbie, just let them have a look. As soon as they get it out it'll feel much better and we can go home,' I pleaded with her.

By now my patience was beginning to wear a little thin. I felt the need to shout, very loud. A curtain being the only thing separating us from the rest of the hospital, I managed to contain myself, trying hard to give the impression that I was a calm, caring mum … which of course I was, a few hours ago. Her over-dramatic behaviour continued for another two hours, and I was feeling more and more embarrassed. Not allowing any nurse or doctor near her, she left them with no choice. The only way they were going to get it out was if they put her to sleep. This seemed ridiculous to me – a stuck earring and she was going to have to have a full-blown anaesthetic. I tried once more in vain to calm her down but it was no use, so the anaesthetic procedure began.

The anaesthetist was lovely. He came to see us and was merrily chatting away to Abbie, who was listening carefully to what he had to say. I think the nurses had clued him up on the situation.

'Do you know what, Abbie? I think this earring has come undone, I think it's falling out!'

He put his hand up to her ear – amazingly, she stayed perfectly still – giving it a quick pull before she realised what was happening, and, hey presto, it was out.

'Yes, that's fantastic. Thank goodness!' I cheered, very nearly giving him a kiss. 'We could have done with you four hours ago!' I said with a huge smile.

Highly relieved that she wasn't going to have the anaesthetic after all and that she'd finally calmed down and shut up, I apologised profusely once more to all the staff, then we snuck out. My ears were burning as we walked back to the car; I feel sure the poor nurses would have been glad to see the back of us. On arriving home, Gary was in the kitchen. As he opened his mouth to speak, I knew what was going to come out, but when he looked at my face he quickly stopped himself. My look of 'Don't you say a word, not a word!' must have been written all over my face. I poured myself a large glass of wine and flopped into the chair. The nurse had given Abbie a badge that read, 'I've been brave at the hospital'. This was extremely kind of her, but a complete lie, and it would have been rather more apt had she given it to me.

James must have flexible bones, as given the amount of falls and accidents he's had over the years, it seems hard to believe he's still never broken anything. A cocktail of skateboarding, free running, waterskiing, surfing and football have each given him plenty of opportunities to do just that, but to date, apart from a sprained ankle, our trips to A&E have been very infrequent.

Perhaps the funniest, although not particularly funny at the time, mishap happened one morning on our way up to school. James was around nine years old and still very much living life in a little world of his own. As his class were going on a school trip that day, he was very excited, but regardless of his excitement we were still running late. He'd been looking for something, as usual just as we'd been ready to leave the house. Then he'd managed to lose one of his shoes. How do you lose one shoe?

Finally, getting out of the door, we realised he'd left his sandwiches on the kitchen worktop. As we were leaving the house for the second time, he asked, 'Mummy please can I get a bottle of pop from the shop?'

'Well, yes, but you're going to have to be quick – we're already late, James. Here's a pound – run ahead. I'll keep walking, you'll have to catch me up.'

He took the pound off me and then turned very quickly and started to sprint towards the shop – not realising that directly in front of him there was a lamp post. Now, the lamp post had been there for as long as I could remember; we'd walked past it quite successfully for several years prior to this morning, but with all the excitement of going on the school trip and me actually letting him have a bottle of pop, he ran straight into it, at full speed. It must have been a real shock to his body, to be completely stopped in its tracks like that. The lamp post did wobble a little, but not quite as much as James. There was a horrible 'thud' sound.

'James, are you okay?' I shouted as I ran over to him, fully expecting him to have been knocked out.

He didn't answer, but he was conscious.

'James, how on earth did you manage that? I think we'd better take you home, you've really taken a knock there.'

'No, Mummy ... please, I want to go on the trip,' he protested.

He started to cry as I examined his injuries. His forehead was quite red from the impact, but he assured me he was fine. What should I do? If I take him home he's going to be so fed up with me, but if I let him go and he's not well? The for and against once more started to have a little tennis match in my brain.

'Please, Mummy, please,' he begged.

'Are you sure you're feeling okay and you still want to go?'

'Yes.'

'Okay, we can go have a word with the teacher, tell her what's happened and see what she thinks.'

We continued our journey to school, James holding on to my hand all the way. On arriving, I explained to his teacher what had happened; she seemed perfectly happy to take him along with them. 'I promise to keep an eye on him, and we'll steer him away from any random lamp posts,' she said with a smile and a shake of her head.

He did have quite a bruise coming out on his forehead at this point but he seemed very proud of it. Apart from that, all did appear to be fine. He made the school trip after all, minus a bottle of pop!

Whilst walking back home I actually saw his pound coin next to the lamp post. I picked it up and went into the shop and bought him some pop for when he returned.

Then there was the time he fell off his skateboard, on to his chin on the concrete. I received a call from one of his friends asking me to come down to the skate park to collect him. Panicking all the way, wondering what state he was going to be in, as apparently he'd fallen from one of the high ramps, I knew then it was going to be a nasty fall. Thank goodness there were no broken bones. He had a swollen and grazed chin but all his teeth and his jaw were intact, and apart from being a bit shaken up he was fine. As accident-prone as James is – and having taken plenty of falls on to his head, shoulder, twisting legs, arms and ankles – he's hardly even needed so much as a plaster, each time bouncing straight back up. I feel sure he would have loved to have worn a pot (that's a cast if you're not from the Yorkshire area), but despite all his efforts, we haven't had a break as yet!

An unfortunate sequence of events led to a nasty accident whilst on holiday in France in 2001 – another holiday with a teenager in tow, but this time she wasn't just angry that we'd taken her away with us on our holiday: she was livid because we'd left her boyfriend behind.

Despite some resistance from Abbie on that morning, it was agreed we were all going for a family bike ride. There was a lovely town about seven miles from where we were staying and Gary had mapped the route out; it would be a distance we could all do. After quite a protest from Abbie, she told us that she would only go if she could wear her earphones and listen to her music. Gary wasn't happy, telling her that if she couldn't hear properly she wouldn't be aware of traffic around her, and other things that could be dangerous. Abbie felt she'd be just fine – and what did he know anyway? He'd had only been cycling for the last forty years!

The journey was very beautiful. The roads were quiet and we didn't see too many cars. We cycled past fields full of sunflowers all facing towards the sun – it was quite impressive. Even Abbie remarked how lovely they were.

Finally, after what seemed like far more than seven miles to me, we passed a signpost with our destination on it. As I was at the front of our peloton, I reached it first and I shouted out to the rest of them, 'Yes, we're here, at last!'

Little did I know that was the worst thing that I could have done, as Abbie who was travelling behind me, half heard what I'd said. Because I was shouting, she thought it must have been something important, so she immediately stopped dead in her tracks to take out her earphones to hear what I was saying. Unbeknown to her, James was travelling quite close behind her, and as we were going downhill he wasn't expecting us to suddenly stop. He went charging into the back of Abbie's bike, sending him flying over the handle-bars, eventually landing in the middle of the road. Gary was at the back to witness the accident but was unfortunately too far away to be able to do anything to stop it happening. Being a fireman he's always pretty calm and laid back when any of the children have any sort of accident, but even he knew this was a nasty one. The only saving grace was that there hadn't been any traffic coming.

However, as James slid down the road on his arm, wearing only a t-shirt, I really didn't know what to expect. Abbie instantly burst into tears, though she wasn't really sure what had just happened. There was a slight delay, then great relief as James began to cry. Gary, by now, had reached him and was carefully checking him for any damage whilst Abbie, myself and James continued to cry. Happily amazed nothing was broken, Gary lifted James on to the grassed area at the side of the road where we examined the damaged arm. There was blood and gravel where skin should have been, but we all breathed a huge sigh of relief that despite the speed, location and lack of protective clothing he was in remarkably good shape. It could have been so much worse.

'When I saw him fly off the bike like that, I was sure we were going to need an ambulance.' Gary couldn't believe it: amazingly after he'd cleaned his arm up, a thin bandage with some antiseptic cream was all that it needed. Once again, his little bones had managed to withstand quite an impact.

Abbie didn't use her earphones on the way back. Nothing was said; she just took it upon herself not to wear them. The upset of it all had proved our point, and she would be the first person to tell anybody now that it's not safe to restrict your hearing whilst riding a bike. You never can be quite sure just what's round that corner.

Words of Wisdom

Accidents will always happen and you can't wrap children up in cotton wool, although I have thought on many an occasion of bubble-wrapping James – but it's just not possible. They can, and will, have accidents whether you're with them or not. Like the rest of us, you're going to feel like a bad parent whenever trouble strikes, but there's often no way you can foresee these things. It's nature's way for them to learn. They get it wrong, it hurts, but they won't do that again. Will they?

34

Taste of their own medicine

Bullies. It doesn't matter where you go, there's one in every school and more than often in every class. This is worth mentioning as it's more than likely to affect most people in some way throughout their lives. It wasn't until Abbie was nine that she had her first taste of bullying. She'd been more than happy with the one best friend up to then. There were the usual strong characters in her class, but she knew to keep well away from them.

In year six a few of the girls in her primary school decided to start up a gang which, unfortunately for her, didn't include Abbie. To make matters worse, her life-long best friend was made part of this group. I believe they told Abbie she couldn't come in because her birthday was in August and they already had a member of the gang with an August birthday – it was as silly as that. But poor Abbie was left out and no longer had her best friend of six years. She went from a perfectly happy little girl, who had always enjoyed school, to a very unhappy, nervous one almost overnight.

We started having tears from her on a morning, and it was so hard saying goodbye in the playground. In fact, there were a few mornings when I let her stay at home with me as I couldn't bare to think of her being left out and unhappy. She didn't want me to go into school and talk to the teacher about it; I'd also offered to have a word with her friend's mum but it was no good – Abbie felt it would only make things worse.

'I really don't think things can get any worse, Abbie. It's worth a try. This is making you so miserable.'

I really felt for her. I remember it only too well. Girl Power at school, when used for all the wrong reasons, is not a good thing; girls can be so cruel and nasty. Lots of the girls fell out with me at school on many an occasion and for no apparent reason other than simply because it was my turn to be bullied; this was usually all down to being, or not being accepted, in a gang. The leader was, without fail, someone who everyone feared. If they told you to do something, you did it, no questions asked, even if it was to fall out with your best friend. Looking back now, that's laughable, but at the time it's your whole world. Often your stomach would be in knots and you couldn't concentrate on anything else. I can even remember not being able to sleep at night, worrying about what was going to happen at school the next day. How cruel that you can be made to feel like that, especially when you've done nothing wrong.

Along with my friends, Alice and Ellen, I had secret plans which helped us all get through those days – the ones when everyone else had fallen out with you: pretending in front of the gang at school not to be friends, but as soon as we arrived home on an evening, we'd be straight on the phone to each other, feeling smug that we'd got one over on the class bully.

Ellen and I lived on the same street, therefore always walked to and from school together, unless, of course, she'd been told not to talk to me. She would then pretend to walk off and leave me, but actually wait around the corner; this was until the ringleaders had boarded their bus home, then as I walked past her she would shout out to me, 'I'm your friend really.'

Looking back, if truth be told, I don't think anyone really liked all the falling out. So why, then, didn't we stand up to these people and say, no, I'll talk to whoever I want to?

The only thing worse than yourself getting bullied at school is knowing your child's being bullied. All you want to do is protect them and stop this from happening, but as you're not with them 24/7 this, I'm afraid, is impossible. Abbie would leave for school on a morning with tears in her eyes. My stomach would be in knots and I'd pray that when she came home that night she may have sorted things with them and they would be friends with her again. But day after day, week after week, it continued.

School may tell you not to retaliate but to go and speak to them about it – but let's face it, we all know that's only going make matters worse: the enemy will hate you even more, because once you've involved the teachers, you're now a 'grass' as well. The teachers may protect you whilst you're at school, but who's going to protect you when you're on your way home?

*

Eventually things did seem to calm down a little for Abbie, but school wasn't the same for her anymore. We were due to move house away from the area just before the end of year six. I'd promised Abbie I'd still bring her over to finish the year out, but she decided to take this opportunity and moved schools for those last few weeks of term in the hope that she might meet some new friends before going to high school the following September.

This proved to be a good move for her as she did make friends with a few of the girls in her class. All was calm until about a year into high school when unfortunately some more bullying raised its ugly head. Abbie was once again reluctant to go to school, and, recognising the signs, I knew something was wrong. Eventually I managed to get out of her what was going on; I was gutted. She begged me not to go into school. So I told her the only way to stop this once and for all was to play them at their own game. Abbie was now twelve and she had been a gymnast since she was eight years old, training for three hours, four times a week. I knew, as little as those arms were there was plenty of strength in them.

'Next time she bothers you, just turn round and punch her once very hard, then walk away. That's all it'll take, Abbie. I promise you she won't bother you again'.

This I had told her time and time again. But she was my daughter and not a fighter, so this wasn't something that would come naturally to her. 'I'll come down there and punch her myself, and if the teachers have a problem with that, I'm quite prepared to speak to them about it.' Not very helpful, I know, but I couldn't help myself when she came home devastated after another difficult day. It was an anger I've never felt before. If I could have gone into school in place of Abbie, I would gladly have done so, sorting out the lot of them.

One day, after numerous other things were being done to her at the hands of these girls –one in particular who, of course, never went anywhere without her entourage closely behind her – Abbie finally gathered up enough rage to fight back. Whilst putting her sandwich box into her locker that morning, she accidentally dropped it and some of her dinner fell on the floor. Unfortunately for Abbie, the timing couldn't have been worse because the girl in question and her tribe were standing right behind her. They instantly took it upon themselves to take this opportunity to stand on her sandwiches and squash her yogurt. Big mistake on their part! Anyone who knows Abbie well would know better than to touch her food, let alone squash it in front of her very eyes. On the plus side, it did provoke her enough to retaliate, because this time they'd over-stepped the mark.

She came home that evening with a huge smile on her face. 'Mum, Mum, I've done it, I've done it. I slapped her right across her face. I didn't even know I was going to do it. It just happened!' Abbie screeched as she came through the door.

Thank goodness my suggestion seemed to have worked. I knew she had it in her; she just needed to get angry enough, and with the four years of gymnastic conditioning under her belt I feel sure there will of been quite some power behind that slap.

'Well done, that's fantastic, darling!' I shouted as I flung my arms around her. 'And, what did she do?'

'She ran off into the toilets, followed by the rest of the gang.'

'Brilliant. What did I tell you?'

This was the best outcome. She was thrilled with herself but probably not quite as thrilled as I was with her. We all spent the next week or so singing the theme tune from *Rocky* to her every time she walked past us. Everyone was so pleased to hear about what she had done, and it was clear to see that her confidence in herself had miraculously returned. Surprisingly, she never had any more problems with that set of girls again, or anyone else in school for that matter.

James, on the other hand, to my knowledge, hasn't had to put up with any real bullying. Boys in general, it would seem, deal with things in a very different way. They don't tend to have the amount of fallings-out that girls do. There are exceptions to the rule, I know, but after going through Abbie's traumas, it did surprise and please me watching James breeze his way through primary school – and so far so good in high school. It always amazed me when he would tell me he was meeting up with some friends in the park. I would notice that it was past the time he'd said he was going.

'James, you shouldn't be here. I thought you were going to the park.'

'Oh, I've changed my mind now. I can't be bothered.'

Having asked him if he'd let anyone know he wasn't going to be there, he would usually say, 'Oh, I'll tell them tomorrow at school.' It wouldn't have been that simple if they'd been girls, now, would it? A full explanation as to why and exactly what was the problem would have been expected, and woe betide them at school the next day if they'd not let anybody know they weren't coming. Boys, in general, seem to just get on with it; there's no hidden agendas with them. They don't appear to waste their time overthinking things.

Words of Wisdom

If only it could be that simple for girls, I feel school would be a much more pleasant experience.

Now, I'm not saying that violence is the way to go – of course it absolutely isn't – but let's be real here: sometimes, with some people, it is the only thing that actually works. Often a taste of their own medicine is exactly what they need.

Our *Rocky* experience with Abbie left us feeling that justice had been done, as finally someone had stood up to the bully of the school. Better still, it was my little girl.

35

The lights are on but there's nobody home

Having bought James a drum kit for his eleventh birthday, for a special treat we invited Tom over with his electric guitar so the boys could have a jamming session together. As Stacey had now moved to York, when they came to see us they often slept over. Phil, her husband, worked away a lot, so when Gary was on nights in the week, we would often get together to sleep at each other's houses. It was nice for the boys, and they'd always got on well with Hannah, Tom's little sister – although as she was now nine, it wasn't quite as much fun for her as it had once been as Abbie was now too old for her to play with, whilst the boys were starting to become boring, no longer happy to play the games she could join in with and instead wanting to play on the PlayStation most of the time. This in mind, we did try to make it more fun for her; she loved Jasper and would spend lots of time playing with him, always wanting to take him for a walk, as long as she could hold him on the lead. As it was January and dark by 3.30, on this occasion we hadn't managed to fit a walk in.

Understandable, then, that Hannah would much rather have been staying at home. Stacey could usually keep her happy with the promise of a McDonalds breakfast on their journey back home the next morning. That said, on this occasion they weren't able to stay over and were going to set off home at about 9pm.

The drums were set up in the dining room, so when he arrived Tom plugged in his electric guitar and they were off. Abbie was not impressed, as you can imagine at sixteen it was probably her worst nightmare.

'Really?' she said to me, with a look on her face that I'd seen far too many times.

'It's his birthday treat, Abbie. It's only for one night,' I shouted over the noise, which was shaking the whole house at this point.

She stormed off up to her bedroom and slammed the door behind her. Stacey and I were trying to have a conversation in the other room but it wasn't easy, and Jasper was trying to bury himself under the sofa. When the phone rang it was not surprising, then, that we didn't hear it. It wasn't until later I noticed the answer phone flashing; when I played it back it was the next-door neighbours.

'Oh no, I bet they're going to complain about the noise,' I said to Stacey in a panic. 'I'd better call them back to explain and apologise.'

When I spoke to them I was very surprised to hear they hadn't heard any noise at all. She was just calling to ask me if we'd been up into our top shed.

'The light's on in your top shed. I was sure you'd told me Gary was working nights, but it looked like there was a man there.'

'No one's been out of the house at all.' My stomach suddenly took a nervous jump.

'Okay, don't worry, I'll send Richard round to have a look.'

Our garden is on a steep slope: it goes up three levels and from our house you can only see the top bit from the upstairs windows. As the shed is on the top level we all quickly ran up in to Abbie's bedroom to see if we could see anything out of the window.

'Turn your light off, Abbie. We need to look out of your window,' I said to her as we all barged in.

'What are you doing?!' she screamed at us.

'I think there's someone breaking into the shed.'

'Really? Wow, let's have a look,' she replied, pushing us all out of the way.

Well, the light was on and the door was wide open, and we certainly hadn't been up there. There was a knock at the door – we all jumped and looked at each other as if to say, 'Who can that be?'

'It'll be Richard from next door. I'll go,' I said, by now feeling rather tense.

I ran down the stairs, Abbie following me, and opened the front door to Richard. 'Thanks so much for coming.'

'No worries, but I'd ring the police as there's still someone up there.'

'Is there? Abbie, you ring the police. Tell them we think someone's still here. I'm going up the garden with Richard.'

The other point with our garden is you can only get in through the side gate, which is at the bottom end of the garden, next to the house. Therefore I can only imagine what they must have thought when they looked in and realised there was a small rock concert going on in our dining room. As it was dark outside we had all the lights on in the house, meaning we couldn't see out but they could see in. This will have made it extremely easy for them to get up the garden path without being seen or heard. As it's the only way in, it's also the only way out, so if they were still up there then they had to come back down the same way.

'You all stay in the house and wait for the police,' I whispered, thinking I was in a Starsky and Hutch film but feeling quite nervous by this point.

Richard and I tiptoed up the garden; he had a baseball bat and I had a rolling pin. My heart was pounding at this point, and I remember thinking, shouldn't we be inside waiting for the police to do this? Anyway, we were nearly at the top of the garden now, so there was no going back. The beer fridge was open and empty! Richard thought he could hear voices in next door's garden and when we looked, our fence had been completely knocked down – it was flat to the ground. So that's how they'd made their escape.

As we were starting to put the pieces together, Abbie shouted up, 'The police are here, Mum.'

We returned to the house to fill them in with what we'd worked out. 'I think they're still in next door's garden,' Richard whispered to them.

'Okay, is everyone inside now? As we can let our dogs go. Do you have a dog?' the policewoman asked us.

'Yes we do, where is Jasper?' I was looking out of the window as I said this when Stacey tapped me on the shoulder and pointed into the living room. There he was, on the sofa, legged out; he hadn't moved the whole time, not even when the police had come to the door! The policewoman smiled and shook her head.

'Okay, yes, everyone's inside the house. You can let the dogs go,' she radioed through.

They released the dogs off into our garden; they were sniffing around, barking and making plenty of noise. Jasper still didn't stir.

Hannah, at this point though, was jumping up and down. 'This is so exciting! Do you think the dogs will catch them?'

'We were just round the corner when we got your call,' the police woman replied. 'Let's hope we arrived here in time, because if they're around, the dogs will find them.'

She continued to ask us some more questions about what we'd been doing and when she looked round and saw the drum kit and electric guitar I think she got the picture.

About half an hour had passed. Radio messages were going back and forth, the kids were getting more and more excited by the second. Even Abbie had stayed out of her room and was intrigued. At one point it was looking like they'd caught them, then the other two police officers returned.

'We were so close. The dogs picked up the scent straight away but they managed to get away through the back gardens. We have some other police looking out for them though, so fingers crossed.'

It looked like we'd probably disturbed them as they'd thrown some of the bottles of wine and beer they'd stolen in next door's garden. Obviously, they couldn't run away fast enough with it. The police took finger prints from the shed, carefully watched by Hannah, who was enjoying every minute. After years of watching Columbo with her mum, she was intrigued. By now there were three policemen in the garden, a policewoman and two more male PCs in the house. The doorbell had been ringing constantly, people were in and out, up and down the garden – and still Jasper hadn't move from his spot on the sofa.

As they were leaving Stacey shouted, 'Don't forget your highly trained sniffer dog here, will you!' She was looking at Jasper.

'Yes, if you ever decide you don't want him anymore there's always a job at our place for him!' the policewoman replied, laughing as she went out the door.

Well, that had certainly livened the evening up a bit, especially for Hannah. 'This has been the best night I've ever had!' she beamed as they were leaving.

'Can't we stay and sleep, Mum? In case they come back again?'

She'd certainly enjoyed her evening playing detective, and this was definitely one evening when I would have much preferred them to be sleeping over.

Words of Wisdom

Always keep your shed locked up, especially if it's got alcohol in it. Maybe holding a small rock concert in my dining room wasn't one of my best ideas to date, but the kids did have a great time. I took my rolling pin up to bed with me that night and, besides, we had Jasper the fearless hound to protect us. A comforting thought!

I think our best deterrent, should we have needed it, would be Abbie the angry teenager. Now, that's someone not to be messed with.

36

Leavers assemblies

If you've not yet been to a leavers assembly then I suggest you brace yourself, as my experiences have left me a little scarred. Usually they fall on the last day before school breaks up for the summer holidays. Because, for the year six pupils, it would be their last day in primary school, this gives it maximum impact. Someone came up with the bright idea that it might be nice to get the kids to do a little performance and invite mums and dads into school to say goodbye. *In theory* a nice idea ... well, you see what you think.

When Abbie was leaving year six and primary school, we were also moving away. It was a daunting thought and a big move, but we'd decided that it was the best time to do this, as Abbie was due to go to upper school whilst James was going to be starting at primary. We'd always lived in this part of Yorkshire, quite close to both our families. Having run the hair salon for the last twenty-three years, we knew plenty of people, so this was never going to be easy.

The dreaded day finally came, and I think I'd been awake most of the night worrying about it, although in hindsight I needn't have bothered. The leavers assembly was to take place that afternoon. Abbie was already at school and she'd told me what was going to happen and what she would be doing, she seemed okay with it – at least that's what I kept telling myself all that day, but it didn't seem to make much difference. Every time I thought about walking into school, all that came to my mind was that this was to be the last time we would ever go there, causing me to instantly well up. By lunchtime I already looked like a bullfrog. I kept calming myself down, but then a few minutes later I'd be off again. Consequently, by the time two o'clock finally arrived I had to make the decision of whether I was going or not. Gary was coming straight from work and I'd arranged to meet him inside. I parked up outside the gates, but the trickling tears had, by then, turned into sobbing. I knew Abbie would have been mortified had I walked in looking like that, as no amount of make-up could disguise the fact that I'd been crying for most of the day. It was no good; I couldn't possibly go in. I didn't – something I've perhaps regretted since, but I really feel at the time that I had no choice, as I wouldn't have been capable of speaking to anyone. So I sat in the car instead and cried a bit more.

An hour later Gary came out, looking puzzled, having enjoyed the concert and not shed so much as a tear. He really couldn't understand what on earth was wrong with me. The difference between men and women, maybe? I must admit perhaps I was bordering slightly on the hysterical side that day. So I'm afraid, and a little ashamed, to say I can't actually tell you what happened at Abbie's leavers assembly except that Gary really enjoyed it. As much as I have regrets for not going to that one, I can, unfortunately, remember all too well what happened at the next leavers assembly seven years later, and on reflection it may have been a good idea to give that one a miss too.

With James being my youngest child, I felt that I really did have to make the effort to be strong this time. I couldn't possibly miss out again. He'd done a full seven years at this little village school. The teachers had been fantastic, especially the headmaster – he was first class, just like a granddad to all the children, knowing each child by name and who their parents were. If he ever saw you either in or out of school it was always 'Hello, Mrs Mitchell'.

He knew each and every pupil and always had time to speak to parents when he needed to. James had loved his time there and was especially fond of his year six teacher.

Once again, the dreaded day arrived. I managed to get a seat at the back of the hall, next to one of the mums I knew pretty well. So it began with the children standing up one by one and telling the audience what they wanted to be when they grew up. This ranged from joining the army to hairdressing and, as I remember this particular week, James said he was going to be a professional skateboarder! It was all very sweet; it got a few laughs around the room and I thought to myself, it's okay, I can do this. Then the teacher announced that at this point he was going to put on his sunglasses. What an earth did he mean? There wasn't any sun coming into the hall. Then, as the lights went off and the projector started up, I remembered a while ago James had asked for a photograph of himself as a baby, along with a more recent one, to take into school. On came the music: It was Adele's *Someone Like You.*

Oh my goodness. It was as if the lyrics had been written just for the assembly. I was devastated.

'I wish nothing, but the best for you.'

Now I knew why the teacher had put his dark glasses on, as he'd seen it before. As the pictures came up one by one of the children as babies followed by a picture of how they looked today, we were all laughing and crying at the same time. It was a painful reminder of how fast the years had flown by. I'd soon worked my way through all the tissues I'd brought – and I'd brought a lot – as the pictures continued to flash up on the screen and Adele carried on singing:

'Don't forget me, I beg, I remember you said, sometimes it lasts in love but sometimes it hurts instead.'

By now the girls in the class were crying (all seven of them), and when I looked over I could see James wiping a tear from his little cheek. I felt like someone was ripping my heart out. I could hardly breathe. There were by now plenty of tears around the room, so at least I wasn't the only one but I do think I might have been slightly more upset than most. It was the end of an era for me. There had been a seven-year age difference in-between my two, so I'd done a full fourteen years of primary school runs, and I'd thoroughly enjoyed every minute of it. I just couldn't believe I wouldn't be doing it anymore.

When the song and pictures of torture finally finished, I was exhausted and dreading the lights coming back on. I didn't want James to see me so upset, and I certainly didn't want to see him upset either. It was too late for that as by now him and the rest of the class were hugging their teacher for the last time – heartbreaking to watch.

Everyone began clapping and then people started to make a move for home. I couldn't speak to any other parents at this point; instead I just sat stunned in my chair for quite some time. I wasn't really sure what to do next; I didn't want to go home or pull James away, but it was inevitable, as the poor teacher would need to leave and go home at some point. I waited as long as I could, being one of the last ones remaining. When I spotted the caretaker standing by the door with his keys in his hand, I knew the time had come. After I had to almost prise James away from his teacher, we said our final goodbyes and set off to walk home, both of us left a little numb by the whole experience.

'That was a lovely assembly, James. Well done,' I managed to squeak as we arrived home.

I was actually meant to be going out that night, though this was the last thing I felt like doing. I felt bereft, and I definitely didn't want to leave James. He was quiet that evening and not too bothered about going out to play with his friends. A day or two later he was back to his usual happy-go-lucky self. As for me, well, here we are now five years on and I still can't listen to that Adele song. If ever it's played on the radio I have to turn it off as quickly as possible as it still brings a lump to my throat.

Words of Wisdom

Ten out of ten to the teacher for lasting memories. James's assembly certainly did that.

As for school times, 8.45 and 3.15, I was lost for quite some time, I can tell you. But five years on, I think I'm just about over it.

37

Too big to be little, too little to be big

As cruel as the teenage years may be, I'm truly convinced there's a perfectly good reason for this; those years are most certainly nature's way to help with the separation process.

We spend around about twelve years with our young children. After the first initial shock when a new baby comes into your life and turns your whole world as you've known it completely upside down, it's surprising how quickly you become accustomed to this new way of life, soon forgetting life before children. Then maybe child number two comes along (some may go on to have a third, fourth, or even more). This is now your life and what you've become. You no longer put yourself first as you once did; your predominant thoughts and actions have your children's happiness, safety and love before anything else. This love is returned to you tenfold from them; they look up to you, respect you and need you more than anyone else in the whole wide world. You've put so much of your time, love and energy into them, and what an exceptional job you've done. You can't possibly imagine anything happening to change that. The thought of them one day growing up and leaving home haunts you and so is kept suppressed at the back of your mind, enabling you to pretend that it's never going to happen. Then, suddenly, often with no prior warning, one night you tuck them into bed a child and they wake up a teenager! So now that little person who's walked beside you holding your hand, looked up to you, hung on to every word you've ever said, laughed at all your jokes and believed all your stories, has decided, almost overnight, that they don't actually need you anymore. You're no longer funny or clever, and the only things you're useful for now are transport and money – I'm afraid it can be that cut and dried. This child that you've nurtured for all these years is suddenly starting to break away from you. You see, nature arranges it this way and makes them so horrible and difficult to live with to ease the transition for you, because, after four to five years of this treatment, believe it or not, not only are you going to be showing them the door but you're actually going to be helping them out with their belongings.

The arguments with Abbie started when she was around twelve years old. I honestly think girls are ruled by hormones from an early age; they don't seem to get much chance to be a child before changes in their bodies and minds start to happen.

This must be taken into consideration before I continue as, to be fair, my own memories of being a teenager are not especially happy ones. One minute you're being told you're not old enough to do certain things, then the next, apparently you have to grow up. Extremely confusing.

For Abbie, having a brother six years younger than her wasn't helpful throughout those teenage years as, according to her, James was, annoying, spoilt and never moved anywhere faster than a snail. These, amongst a lot of other derogatory things, through the eyes of raging hormones, were her descriptions of him.

To be fair, I'll agree with her about him moving through life at a very leisurely pace. It was impossible to rush him in anything he did. You see, Abbie did everything at great speed – she always had done, right from being a toddler – but unfortunately for her, James did not. She couldn't stand to be late for anything, but her speedy ways and obsession with being punctual were destroyed by the fact that James was incapable of doing anything quickly. Well, he wasn't nicknamed Captain Slow for nothing, was he? He spent a lot of his younger days in trouble with Abbie, usually for making her late. I can promise you he wasn't spoilt, but in her eyes he always got away with the things that she never did. As for annoying, he lived in a little world of his own the majority of the time. In my opinion, for what it's worth, he'd learnt from a very young age to stay well out of Abbie's way.

I can remember purposely making excuses to go into my older brother's bedroom, solely to annoy him. James wouldn't have dared do that to Abbie. His inability to move quickly anywhere could be very wearing. He never seemed to grasp the meaning of hurry up, which does surprise me, as at her worst Abbie would often scream into his face, 'Hurry up, or I'm going to kill you!'

I do think, at the time, she meant it, but Captain Slow just seemed to plod along in a world of his own, not at all flustered by her or her threats. Even at the age of ten he could take up to five minutes fastening shoe laces, and that was just one of the shoes. He would always find something to do, or look for, when all the rest of us were standing at the door ready to leave the house. Frustrating for all of us, but to a hormonal teenager, torture, I think!

Our hour-long trips in the car four times a week to take her to gymnastics were not pleasant. Gary would generally be at work, so most evenings I had to take James along with us. Understandably, it was extremely boring for him, so he never wanted to come. After always setting off late, thanks to James, we would then sit nose-to-tail in the teatime traffic.

You could almost see smoke coming out of Abbie's ears as we got later and later and she got more and more stressed. It was always better if she didn't speak at all, but if she did it was usually only to hurl abuse at the world. I found it was best not to venture into any kind of conversation with her at times like that.

However, I do recall once making the big mistake of telling her that her make-up had left an orange line on her chin. Needless to say, I was shot down in flames for this, only to be asked, what did I know about makeup. She'd often switch the car radio on to avoid having to make conversation with us, but usually on to a channel I disliked. Then would follow a frenzied button-pushing episode between us, where we both pressed the radio tuner from Radio 2 to Capital constantly till one of us gave in! This was usually me.

Eventually arriving at the gym club – a great relief to both James and I that we'd survived another gym journey – she would slam the door behind her.

'Thanks for the lift!' I'd sarcastically shout after her.

On returning home that evening, her mood could be quite the opposite: she might be singing and laughing, looking at us all as if to say, what's the matter with you lot? What's your problem now?

Arguing was new to me, as until Abbie had arrived I'd never actually had a proper argument with anyone. Understandably with this in mind, I certainly didn't enjoy it, and I wasn't very good at it either. Abbie, on the other hand, was great at it. She was also pretty good at lying: she could look you in the eye and tell you that black was white. This combination was truly mighty, especially against me as I did then, and still do, believe everything anyone tells me. Was I doing it all completely wrong? Was I really that bad a mother? Maybe I didn't understand her. Was I unreasonable?

It is me, then, I would think as I lay in bed at night going over and over in my mind the day's events. I honestly did start to question myself and truly believe I was to blame. The parenting tennis match would then start in my head once more, going from blaming myself, then in the next breath thinking, don't be ridiculous, she's a teenager. On a bad day, I could easily convince myself I was useless as a mum, whilst on a good day, I would have none of it. This roller-coaster behaviour would slowly start to become normal for Abbie, and on speaking to other mums with teenagers I eventually realised that perhaps I wasn't to blame after all. She could come into a room in a great mood, then walk out of it just a few minutes later furious for no apparent reason. You never knew which Abbie you were going to get.

She and Gary did clash just a little. I'd learnt, as we went along, to let a few things go – it just wasn't worth it sometimes, and, besides, I didn't always have the time or the energy to argue. Abbie was as determined as ever, just as she had been since the day she was born. Gary sometimes found that hard to deal with, probably as he wouldn't back down either; indeed, there has been one or two 'pistols at dawn' sessions between the two of them, and both James and I would make ourselves scarce whilst these were going on. One thing Abbie and Gary did agree on, though, was music. They both enjoyed listening to a lot of the same bands, so a bit of common ground could, if all else failed, be found there.

We were very lucky on the boyfriend front, by all accounts and having spoken to plenty of parents whose daughters and sons have been heartbroken many a time. Abbie met Daniel when she was fourteen and is still with him now. Surprisingly, she became a different person when he was visiting at our house. All of a sudden she was lovely with us all, even James, smiling and talking to us ... anyone would have thought she actually liked us. Having a boyfriend from an early age also meant she wasn't too bothered about going out and getting drunk with her friends – something else that can be a great worry to us parents. She definitely had her moments, but in the grand scale of things, I truly feel that we got off very lightly.

Despite the six-year gap not always being ideal when they were little, it did have its advantages as we approached the teenaged years, as when James hit puberty Abbie was coming out of the other side. My heart goes out to any parents living with more than one hormonal teenager in the house at once.

Boys seem to get much longer to play and be children. When James was twelve I'll never forget a friend of his, Robbie, coming over to see him. Robbie was fifteen; they would usually sit on the PlayStation together, but on this occasion James had just had a birthday and had received a new set of Nerf guns. So, instead of sitting staring at a screen, for a change they were running round the house playing war games. I'd happily left them to it and was busy pottering, tidying upstairs and putting washing away. As I came down the steps I had to step over Robbie as he'd barricaded himself behind a wall of cushions from the sofa. James was hiding across the hall, armed with a Nerf gun, waiting patiently until Robbie moved so he could start to fire at him. Robbie was so transfixed with the game he didn't even notice me sneaking past with the washing pile under my arm. He then proceeded to drag himself, with his elbows, across the laminate floor into the hall way, ninja-style, in an attempt to get closer to James unnoticed. I stopped in my tracks and watched for a while. As they were both completely lost in their game of make-believe, by now they were firing Nerf bullets at each other and throwing themselves about the house, generally having a great time. It was quite refreshing to watch and brought a smile to my face. Robbie was already a good foot taller than me, and there was no doubt he was definitely growing up into a young man, but I think this was a sure sign that he wasn't quite ready to completely let go of his childhood.

James, when he hit the teenage stage, was totally different from Abbie: not quite as vocal, though the PlayStation sulk was soon to become the cause of many an argument in our house. Any time spent on the PlayStation usually resulted in either banging and clattering from his bedroom as he threw the controls down in a paddy, or hours spent calling him down for tea only to be answered by 'I'll be down in a minute, I'll just get past this level.' Several minutes/hours later, you're still waiting! Abbie had never bothered with the games side of technology; her mobile had always been her priority, but from what I've seen, boys with their games can become quite obsessed – to the point where a perfectly calm well-mannered young man can turn into Mr Angry after just a few minutes of playing on a game. We tried many different ways to police his time spent on the console: Giving him a time limit of about two hours a day – but unless you're there all day to manage it, with the best will in the world that's not going to happen. I often threaten to go up and switch it off, but all I would get was 'No, Mum, you can't. I'm in a game with my mates, and you'll cancel it all.' To be honest, I wasn't sure whether it would or not, so I never dared to turn it off. Oh, and there was the small detail of me actually having no idea then, or now, of how to switch it off.

Gary knew how though, and he did turn it off on a number of occasions. Then followed some pretty nasty arguments between the two of them, and as James was now becoming bigger and stronger the language wasn't really to my taste, as in James's frustration a few choice words would sneak out, which didn't go down well with Gary at all. James would go through different stages with his PlayStation; it was either all or nothing. One minute he'd want to be playing it all the time and we couldn't get him to come out with us or do anything else; a few weeks later, he didn't seem interested, never even switched it on. So we did at least get a reprieve from time to time from the tantrums – until another new game came out ... then, I'm afraid, the whole process would start again. It was without a doubt that after a session on his PlayStation James was a different person for a good while. Whether he had won or not, he would always be frustrated and angry; this has always been a mystery to me.

'It's just a game, James. What's wrong with you?' (Perhaps the wrong thing to say, but I couldn't help myself sometimes.)

Apart from this, and him not being very organised and usually late for most things, James is still plodding along nice and steady through the teenage years, growing at an amazing rate, to the degree where I can almost see a difference in him each morning when he comes down the stairs, and consequently eating me out of house and home. I could probably write a whole book on the teenage years alone, but I must stop there as my original plan was to have this finished whilst my children were still living at home with me.

Words of Wisdom

Yes, nature tries very hard to make the separation process a little easier for us parents. There's no real way round it – you just have to put your head down and keep going till you come out of the other side. And you will – maybe a little bruised, but certainly the wiser for it, as changes are inevitable, whether you're ready or not. Abbie's now in her twenties and I can laugh with her about some of the things she did and said over the years. I've got my first badge for completing seven years with a teenager, but I'm not finished yet as I've still got another four to go with James.

Advice so far, from where I'm sitting: once you accept that the little sweetheart you've raised until now, to the best of your ability, is out of your hands and possibly your control, try not to beat yourself up about it too much. Just know they're not purposely going out of their way to upset you, although at times it may seem like they are. It's only their hormones taking over, and they honestly can't help themselves.

They're too young to do some things but too old to do others. So where do they fit in? Well they don't, and that's the problem. My only comfort here is to tell you to sit tight, as they will come back again, eventually, and then all that hard work that you've put in from birth will slowly start to shine through once more.

38

Perfect mum?

So, do you know who I am now? I think you probably do.

I'm no Super-Mum or anything out of the ordinary. I didn't have three, four, or even six children. Just the two ...

But whether you have the one child or twelve children it's still the same, and it's taken me twenty-one years to realise what you don't teach your children, they will, without a doubt, teach you. They don't come along into our lives with an instruction manual, so it's all pretty much down to us to muddle on through and to just get on with it to the best of our abilities. Which is exactly where I'm coming from, because there's no real right or wrong way to do it.

You may look around you at other mums and think, oh look at her, she's got it all sussed, but she's probably looking at you thinking exactly the same. You see, your job as a mum is constantly changing, so just when you're getting the hang of babies, they become toddlers, then the toddlers are suddenly children, and before you know it, you're living alongside a teenager. So, without even realising it, we move on to the next stage with no prior training – how amazing is that? This continues throughout their lives, and you certainly can't rely on them all being the same for some guidance, as, whether they're brothers, sisters or even twins, they are all so very different.

Tonight, as I sit by the swimming pool watching my youngest – who's now fourteen years old – having his diving lesson, his body now slightly starting to resembling that of a man, I'm relieved to be able to report that he no longer bites his best friend. This, as with many other worries, has now been left long behind us, leaving plenty of room for new worries, which will come and go. I'm glad I've realised before it's too late that when it comes to bringing up children you have to go with whatever feels right for you. So now, instead of beating myself up about things, I can smile and know I'm doing my best.

I hope that by sharing just a few of our family's little stories, it's helped to reassure you that no one's journey is smooth. I wanted to fill you in on some of the everyday occurrences that can and will crop up in your life with children, usually when you're least expecting it. They're the things that all the books on bringing up children don't tell you about and I especially wanted to let you know, just in case you were wondering, that no one is perfect. We all doubt and question ourselves constantly, worrying if we've made the right decision, been too soft, too firm or just got it completely wrong. The answer to this is yes, we've all done every one of these things, but in-between, there are also plenty of times when we've got it absolutely right too.

So whether you're breastfeeding, chasing toddlers around or screaming at teenagers, I hope this has been of some help to you. If it's done nothing besides made you chuckle, then I'm happy with that. My only true advice that I feel I'm qualified to give you would be to laugh: laugh as much as you can, whether things are going right, wrong or you're not too sure what else to do. This technique has been tried and tested by myself and all my friends, and I can guarantee it works. I feel very lucky to be sharing my journey with fantastic friends and family who have laughed with me, at me ... and not minded me laughing at them.

The wise, older ones will have said to you on plenty of occasions, like they have said to me, 'Make the most of it, because they grow up so fast.'

Perhaps now I'm an old wise one too, because there is in fact just one more suggestion I have for you: Every now and then, stop, sit down, take a good look at them and what they're doing right now. Enjoy this moment, however big or small it may seem.

When the nights seem endless because your little one is keeping you awake crying all night, or you can't get to sleep because it's three in the morning and your teenager's still not home, please know that you're not alone because there are plenty of other mums all over the world doing that very same thing, right now, with you. You know, it really is the ups and the downs that make your story, so make it a good one – one you can look back on with fond memories and, I hope, a lot of laughter.

Some nights you'll go to bed thinking, not sure I got it quite right today ... but then there will be plenty of other times when you'll be smiling to yourself and thinking, hey do you know what? I am the perfect mum ...

Lightning Source UK Ltd.
Milton Keynes UK
UKOW03f0624190417
299386UK00001B/9/P